SUPERLATIVE EMIRATES

Published and distributed worldwide by
DAAB MEDIA GMBH
Scheidtweilerstrasse 69
50933 Cologne/Germany
fon: + 49 221 690 48 210
fax: + 49 221 690 48 229
www.daab-media.com

Join our community
www.edaab.com and present your work to a worldwide audience

Edited by Caroline Klein
Concept by Ralf Daab
Corporate Design by Meiré und Meiré, Cologne
Layout by Sonia Mion, Nicola Iannibello, Milan
www.ventizeronove.it

Copy Editors: Caroline Klein, Milan; Christiane Blass, Cologne;
Yvonne Courtney, London

German translations by Norma Kessler, Aschaffenburg; Rainer Remmel, Berlin;
Michael Wachholz, Berlin
English translation by Gaines Translations, Frankfurt/Main
Copy proofreading by Michael Konze, Cologne; First Edition Translations Ltd,
Cambridge
Lithography by fgv Group, Milan
www.fgvgrafica.it

Printed in Italy
www.graficheflaminia.com

ISBN 978-3-942597-08-1

SUPERLATIVE
EMIRATES

THE NEW DIMENSION
OF URBAN DESIGN

Edited by CAROLINE KLEIN

Burj Khalifa, Dubai 2010

CONTENT / INHALT

2   IMPRINT

8   INTRODUCTION
     2002–2012 UAE: A Decade of Enlightenment.
     How a Small Arab Nation Captivated the
     World, by Behr Champana Gagneron

16   FACTS

20   AEDAS
     Boulevard Plaza, Dubai
     Dubai Metro, Dubai
     Empire Tower, Abu Dhabi
     Pentominium, Dubai
     U-Bora Towers, Dubai

32   ARCHGROUP CONSULTANTS
     Emirates Park Towers Hotel, Dubai

36   ASYMPTOTE ARCHITECTURE
     The Yas Hotel, Abu Dhabi
     Strata Tower, Abu Dhabi

46   ATKINS
     Atrium City, Dubai
     DIFC Lighthouse Tower, Dubai
     X-Change Gateway, Dubai
     Iris Bay, Dubai

56   DBI DESIGN
     Etihad Towers, Abu Dhabi

60   DXB-LAB
     Code Business Tower, Dubai

66   GODWIN AUSTEN JOHNSON
     National Federal Council – New Parliament
     Building Complex, Abu Dhabi

70   ZAHA HADID ARCHITECTS
     Signature Towers, Dubai
     Sheikh Zayed Bridge, Abu Dhabi
     Opus Office Tower, Dubai

86   GLENN HOWELLS ARCHITECTS
     55°TimeDubai, Dubai

92   LAVA
     Snowflake Tower, Abu Dhabi

96   MASDAR CITY, Abu Dhabi

     100   FOSTER+PARTNERS
           Masdar Masterplan

     104   FOSTER+PARTNERS
           Masdar Institute

     108   LAVA
           Masdar Plaza

112 SAADIYAT CULTURAL DISTRICT, Abu Dhabi

     116   ATELIERS JEAN NOUVEL
           Louvre Abu Dhabi

     120   TADAO ANDO
           Maritime Museum

     122   FOSTER+PARTNERS
           Zayed National Museum

     126   GEHRY PARTNERS
           Guggenheim Abu Dhabi

     128   ZAHA HADID ARCHITECTS
           Performing Arts Centre

     130   ASYMPTOTE ARCHITECTURE
           Guggenheim Contemporary
           Art Pavilions

     132   STUDIO PEI ZHU
           Art Pavilion

136 | OMA
City in the desert, Ras Al Khaimah
Rak Jebel Al Jais Mountain Resort,
Ras Al Khaimah
Waterfront City, Dubai

146 | ONL
Manhal Oasis, Abu Dhabi
Al Nasser Group Corporate Headquarters,
Abu Dhabi
Abu Dhabi Automotive Complex, Abu Dhabi

154 | QUANTUM-AIP
Arabian Film Institute Complex, Dubai
Executive Waterfront Residential Island
Complex, Dubai
Bio Research and Development Institute,
Dubai
Corniche Museum and Hospitality Complex,
Abu Dhabi

160 | REISER + UMEMOTO
O - 14, Dubai
Aeon, Dubai

170 | RMJM
Capital Gate Tower, Abu Dhabi

176 | SCHWEGER ASSOCIATED ARCHITECTS
Dubai Pearl, Dubai

180 | SOM
Burj Khalifa, Dubai
Infinity Tower, Dubai
Rolex Tower, Dubai

192 | SMAQ
Xeritown, Dubai

198 | ADRIAN SMITH + GORDON GILL
ARCHITECTURE
Meraas Tower, Dubai
1 Dubai, Dubai
Za'abeel Energy City, Dubai
Park Gate, Dubai

210 | STUDIED IMPACT
10MW Tower, Abu Dhabi

214 | X-ARCHITECTS
Mosque, Abu Dhabi
Museum of Religious Tolerance, Dubai
The White Hotel, Abu Dhabi

222 | ESSAYS

224 | THE VERTICAL DREAM
by Michael Schindhelm

228 | DUBAI AND ABU DHABI:
Identity through imagery,
islands and an architecture of extremes
by George Katodrytis

232 | SUPERLATIVE URBANITY:
The UAE's adventures
in sustainable city making
by Amer A. Moustafa

238 | INDEX

239 | BIBLIOGRAPHY

240 | PHOTO CREDITS

The Palm Jumeirah Island. Dubai 2007

2002 – 2012 UAE:

A Decade of Enlightenment. How a Small Arab Nation Captivated the World.

~ A BRIEF HISTORY

Prior to independence, the United Arab Emirates was Trucial Oman (also known as the Trucial States) and the component sheikhdoms of the territory had been under British protection since 1892. Each sheikhdom was autonomous and followed the traditional form of an Arab monarchy, with each ruler having absolute power over his subjects. In 1952, the Trucial Council, comprising the rulers of the seven sheikhdoms, was established to facilitate common administrative policies, so leading to a federation of the states. Petroleum, the key to the area's future prosperity, was first discovered beneath the coastal waters of Abu Dhabi in 1958. Commercial exploitation began in 1962, subsequently providing substantial revenues. In 1968, Britain announced its intention of withdrawing its military forces from the area by 1971. Later that year, the six Trucial States – Abu Dhabi, Dubai, Sharjah, Umm Al Quwain, Ajman and Fujairah – agreed on a federal constitution to achieve independence as the UAE on 2 December 1971. Ras Al Khaimah joined the following year.

~ FROM MIRAGE TO REALITY

Fast forward to 2004 and the years that have followed, and the UAE – in particular Dubai – has made its mark on the world map, with an unprecedented explosion of ambitious property developments and construction projects. This has been history in the making of gargantuan proportions. Dubai has caught the attention of the developed world as the new land of opportunity. "Build, and they will come!" was again the word on the streets. The incredible volume of construction flourished to such an extent that its workers accounted for most of Dubai's 1.2 millions population. The speed of execution (work continued round the clock) and technological marvels associated with the resulting architecture were astonishing, particularly when many engineering specialists regarded these mega-structures as "impossible". New advancements were being created in civil engineering, architecture, structural formulations and construction management. Building methodologies were redefined for speed, efficiency and safety. Dubai became an experimental ground thanks to the sheer size and scope of these architectural marvels that had never been previously attempted. An architectural playground on the global stage, Dubai became the land of "high risk, high reward" stakes for developers, architects and builders. The world's professionals beat a path to Dubai's door, all jostling to compete and reinvent themselves, their standards, and their ways of doing business. The tiny desert state of just a few decades ago has transformed into a glittering metropolis, technologically advanced, with the world's tallest skyscrapers, the most successful airport, and a unique archipelago of man-made islands that can be viewed from space. It was clear that Dubai's ambitions were not mere mirage but have become reality!

~ DUBAI – THE MAXIMUM CITY

The Dubai government's decision to diversify from a trade-based, oil-reliant economy to one that was service and tourism-oriented instantly made property more attractive and profitable, resulting in an extraordinary property boom. Between 2004 and 2008, the growth of Dubai accelerated with huge civil infrastructure and building projects all over the Emirate. With its "can do" attitude, Dubai attracted thousands of entrepreneurs and professionals from all over the world, who were keen to set up new businesses and make a new life in the city. Properties were released for sale before they had even been built, only to be resold at a significant premium. Rentals soared – with prices outstripping rates in New York and London – due to increasing demand from Dubai's booming population. The Dubai government was eventually forced to introduce a rent increase cap, to curb the flow of residents moving to neighbouring Emirates and commuting to jobs in Dubai. Interest from other Gulf countries was considerable, with oil-rich investors from Saudi Arabia and Kuwait attracted by the Emirate's relaxed lifestyle, as well as buyers from India, Pakistan, Iran, Europe and the UK – all flocked to the tiny Emirate for a slice of the action.

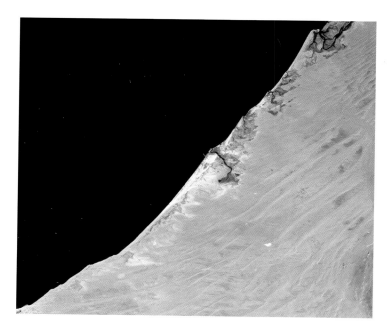

1973

1990

~ THE EMIRATES – DREAM SPIRALS

The global economic downturn resulted in Dubai consolidating its plans for more sustainable growth. The Emirate has been evolving towards a wider reality of its dream – with greater market diversification as developers in the other Emirates were also coming up with their own innovative projects. Revised property laws to help regulate the sale and lease of land and buildings to citizens and expatriates has further helped to stabilise and effectively reboot the property market.

As the UAE capital and the wealthiest Emirate, Abu Dhabi's government had begun to invest heavily in expanding the economy from oil and gas production to business and general tourism, retail and other leisure pursuits. This was set out in the forward-thinking Abu Dhabi Economic Vision 2030 plan, developed by the Abu Dhabi Urban Planning Council. It targets making Abu Dhabi's economy sustainable and not dependent on one particular source of revenue. The development of tall buildings was encouraged which will result in a new skyline of towers over the next couple of decades. With a spectacular waterfront corniche, the city is already known for such architectural landmarks as the Emirates Palace Hotel, the Sheikh Zayed Mosque (currently the eighth largest mosque in the world), not to mention the mega-developments planned for Lulu and Yas Islands and the sustainable, zero-carbon Masdar City. A cosmopolitan city with close to 900,000 inhabitants, its rapid urbanisation brought up particularly ambitious cultural plans – notably the construction of Saadiyat Island Cultural District which aims to become Abu Dhabi's cultural hub.

In contrast, Ras Al Khaimah's government is focusing on the increasing demand for residential properties and high-end tourist resorts in harmony with its natural and ecological assets. With Dubai's high land and property values, Ras Al Khaimah has developed attractive new residential communities, a flourishing free trade zone, modern business parks and various hospitality and tourist attractions.

The Emirate of Sharjah attempted to follow Dubai's lead in property development; however, its impressive array of cultural museums and educational projects is what sets it apart from its neighbours. In 1998 it won the prestigious UNESCO award as the cultural capital of the Arab region. Prior to the global economic crisis in 2008, Sharjah was experiencing the front-end cycle of the property boom, due to its lower rents and property prices which attracted residents from the more expensive Dubai and Abu Dhabi. Ongoing proposed developments include the Nujoom Islands projects.

Ajman, the smallest Emirate with just 260 km² of land, has a long coastal boundary, giving it a unique setting of its own. In 2004, the UAE government declared the area a freehold, giving it desirable real estate investment prospects. Up until 2008, Ajman's real estate had been thriving, with some major developments being realised, becoming one of the biggest revenue generators and profit-disbursing areas in the UAE. To date, developers in Ajman have announced mostly residential and freehold property projects such as the Al Naeymiyah Towers, Al Khor Towers, Uptown Ajman and Ajman One.

Under existing property law regulating land and property ownership in Umm Al Quwain, property ownership is limited to UAE nationals. Having identified the property, tourism and trade industries as its potential growth sectors, developers are investing in real estate projects, with the most prominent proposal being Al Salaam City.

The influx of expatriates into Fujairah is reflected by its rapid economic development. Strong demand for low-cost housing and office space has resulted in private investment pouring into its construction sector. With Fujairah Tower the tallest landmark, the nature-inspired mountain-sea Mina Al Fajer Resort may well provide the Emirate with a new niche market in luxury hospitality.

Whether many of these initiatives will be built or completed during the current economic climate remains to be seen, but clearly the governing bodies of the UAE continue to respect each other's ambitions, while rising as one united country, with one national identity.

2000

2002

~ BEYOND 2012 – ON THE DREAM OF FOREVER

For more than three decades, oil and global finance drove the UAE's economy. In 2008, the global banking crisis, falling oil prices and collapsing real estate prices hit the UAE especially hard. Effects of the economic downturn can still be seen in 2011 – with many large developers in Dubai and Abu Dhabi seeking financial assistance from the UAE government or looking to renegotiate debts with their creditors, many of which are government-owned entities. The economic downturn has led to a severe tightening of available credit that has battered the real estate sector, reducing property values in the Middle East by nearly 50%. However, the high oil prices, favourable demographics, improving standards of living, increasing affordability, and $1.35 trillion worth of planned civil building projects in the GCC countries will help to drive property development over the coming decade. The UAE economy is forecasted to grow by an average rate of 3 to 4% over the next two years, led by stable oil prices and robust non-oil sectors such as construction, infrastructure, financial services, and real estate. Led by the construction of the UAE nuclear power plant and the Emirates Railway project, $29 billion worth of infrastructure projects are set to begin in 2011 – opening business opportunities for the construction and affiliated industries. The Abu Dhabi government has pledged more than $20 billion worth of contracts for the nuclear power plant and an additional $11 billion for the country's railway network. These high-investment projects will undoubtedly boost the expansion and diversification of the UAE's economy, so providing strong momentum for the country's real estate sector.

Innovation in construction requires powerful drivers of new building techniques and applications, new materials, advanced erection fastening technologies, piling and foundation systems. Creative construction management together with talented people and a positive society will enable the country to flourish. In the UAE, developers, contractors and architects have had to develop a culture of innovation in order to create and then survive in a highly competitive market. The results were developments and construction feats that to this day remain unsurpassed and unparalleled – such as the unique hexagonal structural buttressed core and engineering challenges of the Burj Khalifa, developing concrete mixes and curing techniques that could withstand the extreme pressure of the massive building weight and be delivered at record heights, and the logistics and speed of the 210,000,000 m^3 of rock, sand and limestone reclaimed to build the Palm Jumeirah Island. In the last decade, this tiny Arab nation has inspired both its Emirati neighbours and the rest of the world with its limitless vision, and contributed with superlative new dimensions in urbanism – which will influence future generations for years to come.

[Behr Champana Gagneron]

2002 – 2012 VAE:

Ein Jahrzehnt der Aufklärung. Wie eine kleine arabische Nation die Welt faszinierte.

~ GESCHICHTLICHER ÜBERBLICK

Vor ihrer Unabhängigkeit hießen die VAE Befriedetes Oman oder Vertragsküste (Trucial States). Die einzelnen Scheichtümer des Gebiets befanden sich seit 1892 unter britischem Protektorat und waren innerhalb des Verbundes autonom. Sie wurden in der Tradition arabischer Monarchien regiert, die dem Herrscher praktisch absolute Verfügungsgewalt über seine Untertanen verlieh. Im Jahr 1952 wurde der Trucial Council gegründet, dem die Herrscher der sieben Scheichtümer angehörten. Dieser Rat sollte, als Vorstufe zu einer Föderation, der Abstimmung einer gemeinsamen Politik in administrativen Fragen dienen. Erdöl, Grundlage des heutigen Wohlstands der Region, wurde 1958 zuerst unter den Küstengewässern des nahegelegenen Abu Dhabi entdeckt. Die kommerzielle Nutzung dieser Ressourcen begann 1962 und sorgte für einen drastischen Zuwachs der staatlichen Einnahmen. Im Januar 1968 kündigte Großbritannien an, seine Streitkräfte bis 1971 abzuziehen. Bis Mitte des Jahres 1971 einigten sich die sechs Vertragsstaaten Abu Dhabi, Dubai, Sharja, Umm al-Kaiwain, Ajman und Fujaira auf eine föderale Verfassung, mit dem Ziel, am 2. Dezember 1971 als Vereinigte Arabische Emirate unabhängig zu werden. Erster Präsident wurde Scheich Zayed von Abu Dhabi. Ras al-Khaima schloss sich im Februar 1972 der Föderation an.

~ VON DER VISION ZUR WIRKLICHKEIT

Ein Sprung in die heutige Zeit – in die Jahre seit 2004 – macht deutlich, wie sehr die VAE, insbesondere Dubai, die Weltkarte durch beispiellose Erschließungprojekte und einen ungeheuren Bauboom verändert haben. In gigantischen Ausmaßen wird in dieser Region gegenwärtig Geschichte geschrieben. Dubai erregte das Aufsehen der Industriestaaten und galt bald als das neue Land der unbegrenzten Möglichkeiten: „Baue, und sie werden kommen!" wurde in den VAE erneut zu einem geflügelten Wort. Die Bauprojekte nahmen derartige Ausmaße an, dass Bauarbeiter bald den größten Teil der 1,2 Millionen Einwohner von Dubai ausmachten. Die Geschwindigkeit, mit der man die Projekte ausführte – oft wurde rund um die Uhr gebaut –, und die technischen Meisterleistungen, die die Verwirklichung der architektonischen Entwürfe oftmals erst möglich machten, versetzten die Welt in Staunen, vor allem wenn zahlreiche Ingenieurberater diese Mega-Bauten zuvor als „nicht realisierbar" eingestuft hatten. Auf allen Ebenen des Hochbaus, der Architektur, der Tragsystem-Entwicklung und des Baumanagement wurden neue Maßstäbe gesetzt. Um den neuen Anforderungen an Geschwindigkeit, Effizienz und Sicherheit gerecht zu werden, entstanden spezielle Baumethoden. Dubai entwickelte sich angesichts der schieren Größe und Vielzahl der Projekte zu einem Experimentierfeld für architektonische Wunderwerke, wie sie niemals zuvor in Angriff genommen worden waren. Als globale Spielwiese der Architektur wurde Dubai zu einem Land, das Objektentwicklern, Architekten und Bauunternehmern gleichzeitig enorme Risiken aufbürdete und riesige Erfolgschancen versprach. Wer in der Welt der Architektur und des Bauens einen Namen hatte oder sich einen verdienen wollte, drängte nach Dubai, um mit seinesgleichen zu konkurrieren, um sich neu zu erfinden, neue Maßstäbe zu setzen und innovative Geschäftsideen an den Mann zu bringen. Vor wenigen Jahrzehnten noch ein kleines Emirat in der Wüste, hat Dubai sich in eine glitzernde Metropole verwandelt, auf modernstem technischenen Stand, mit den höchsten Hochhäusern der Welt, dem größten Flughafen und einem Archipel künstlicher Inseln, der in seinem Ausmaß einzigartig und sogar aus dem Weltall sichtbar ist. Die ehrgeizigen Visionen Dubais, soviel steht fest, waren keine Fata Morgana – sie sind längst Wirklichkeit geworden!

~ DUBAI – STADT DER SUPERLATIVE

Die Entscheidung der Regierung von Dubai, die hauptsächlich auf dem Handel mit Öl fußende Wirtschaft des Landes zu diversifizieren und einen Dienstleistungs- und Tourismussektor aufzubauen, führte innerhalb kurzer Zeit zu erheblichen Steigerungen der Nachfrage und der Profitabilität von Grundstücken und Gebäuden und löste bald einen enormen Immobilienboom aus. Von 2004 bis 2008 erlebte Dubai eine intensive Wachs-

tumsphase, die durch gewaltige Infrastrukturmaßnahmen und Bauprojekte in den gesamten Emiraten angeheizt wurde. Die „Alles ist machbar"-Atmosphäre Dubais zog Tausende von Unternehmern und Fachleuten aus der ganzen Welt an, die es eilig hatten, Geschäfte in der Stadt zu gründen und sich eine neue Existenz aufzubauen. Neue Gebäude wurden zum Verkauf angeboten, noch bevor sie gebaut waren, und schon kurze Zeit später mit kräftigem Aufschlag weiterveräußert. Die Mieten schossen angesichts der steigenden Nachfrage durch die rasch wachsende Bevölkerung in die Höhe und übertrafen bald das Preisniveau von New York und London. Die Regierung von Dubai sah sich schließlich gezwungen, Mietpreissteigerungen gesetzlich zu begrenzen, um die Abwanderung von Einwohnern in benachbarte Emirate und eine parallele Zunahme der Pendlerzahlen einzudämmen. Auch seitens anderer Golfstaaten war das Interesse groß. Mit Öl reich gewordene Investoren aus Saudi-Arabien und Kuwait zog es wegen der größeren gesellschaftlichen Freizügigkeit in die Emirate, und auch aus Indien, Pakistan, Iran, Großbritannien und vom europäischen Kontinent strömten Käufer in die winzigen Scheichtümer, um ihrerseits einen Teil vom Kuchen der Geschäfte und des guten Lebens abzubekommen.

~ DIE EMIRATE – HOCHFLIEGENDE TRÄUME
Die globale Wirtschafts- und Finanzkrise führte dazu, dass Dubai seine Planungen konsolidierte und stärker auf ein nachhaltiges Wachstum ausrichtete. Das Emirat weitete seine Vision einer diversifizierten Wirtschaft auf neue Bereiche aus, und auch in den anderen Emiraten legten Investoren innovative Planungskonzepte vor. Eine Überarbeitung der Eigentumsgesetze mit dem Ziel, den Verkauf und das Verpachten von Grundbesitz und Gebäuden an Staatsbürger – auch an solche, die im Ausland leben – neu zu regeln, trug dazu bei, den Immobilienmarkt zu stabilisieren und wieder anzukurbeln.

Als das wohlhabendste Emirat, in dem auch die Hauptstadt der VAE ihren Sitz hat, hatte die Regierung von Abu Dhabi begonnen, sich von

der Erdöl- und Erdgasförderung unabhängiger zu machen und in großem Stil in den Dienstleistungssektor, Einzelhandel, allgemeinen Tourismus sowie spezialisiertere Freizeitbranchen zu investieren. Dargelegt wurde diese Zukunftsplanung in der „Abu Dhabi Economic Vision 2030", die vom Abu Dhabi Urban Planning Council erarbeitet worden war. Das Ziel ist, Abu Dhabis Wirtschaft auf eine nachhaltige Grundlage zu stellen und aus der Abhängigkeit von einer einzigen Einnahmequelle zu befreien. Zur „Vision 2030" gehört auch die Erschließung durch weitere Hochhäuser; das Entstehen einer neuen Skyline in den nächsten Jahrzehnten ist zu erwarten. Die spektakuläre Küstenstraße der Stadt ist schon jetzt für ihre architektonischen Wahrzeichen berühmt, darunter das Emirates Palace Hotel und die Scheich-Zayed-Moschee (gegenwärtig das achtgrößte muslimische Gotteshaus der Welt), ganz zu schweigen von den geplanten Megaprojekten Lulu Island, Yas Island und der nachhaltigen, CO_2-neutralen Masdar City. Im Zuge der rapiden Urbanisierung hat sich Abu Dhabi zu einer weltoffenen Metropole mit nahezu 900.000 Einwohnern entwickelt, deren kulturelle Ambitionen höchst ehrgeizig sind. Davon zeugt vor allem der im Bau befindliche Saadiyat Island Cultural District, der das kulturelle Zentrum Abu Dhabis werden soll.

Im Gegensatz dazu konzentriert sich die Regierung von Ras al-Khaima auf den wachsenden Bedarf an Wohneigentum und luxuriösen Ferienanlagen, der mit den natürlichen und ökologischen Gegebenheiten des Landes in Einklang gebracht werden soll. Angesichts der hohen Immobilienpreise in Dubai hat Ras al-Khaima in attraktive neue Wohnanlagen, eine Freihandelszone, moderne Gewerbeparks und diverse andere Attraktionen für Besucher und Touristen investiert.

Das Emirat Sharja versuchte, dem Beispiel von Dubais Erschließungspolitik zu folgen, doch es setzt sich heute vor allem durch seine eindrucksvolle Ansammlung von Museen und Bildungseinrichtungen von seinen Nachbarn ab. 1998 gewann Sharja die renommierte UNESCO-Auszeichnung zur „Kulturhauptstadt der arabischen Welt". Bis zur Wirtschaftskrise 2008 erlebte das Emirat noch die Anfänge eines neuen Immobilienbooms,

denn die niedrigeren Mieten und Immobilienpreise zogen zunehmend Bewohner aus dem deutlich teureren Dubai oder Abu Dhabi an. Zu den im Bau oder in der Planung befindlichen Anlagen gehört das Projekt Nujoom Islands.

Ajman, das kleinste der Emirate mit nur 260 km² Fläche, verfügt durch seine lange Küstenlinie über eine einzigartige natürliche Umgebung. Die Regierung der VAE öffnete das Gebiet 2004 für den freien Grundbesitz, um es für Investoren attraktiv zu machen. Bis 2008 verzeichnete die Immobilienbranche von Ajman große Zuwächse und konnte die Realisierung mehrerer Großprojekte für sich verbuchen. Sie entwickelte sich zu einer der wichtigsten Einkommensquellen der VAE und produzierte bedeutende Gewinne. Bei den gegenwärtig laufenden Projekten handelt es sich überwiegend um Wohnanlagen für den freien Grundbesitz, zum Beispiel die Al Naeymiyah Towers, Al Khor Towers, Uptown Ajman und Ajman One.

In Umm al-Kaiwain beschränken die bestehenden Gesetze den Besitz von Immobilien auf Bürger der VAE. Immobiliengeschäfte, Tourismus und Handel gelten als die Hauptwachstumsbereiche des Emirats; zu den herausragenden Investitionsprojekten im Immobiliensektor gehört die Al Salaam City. Im Emirat Fujaira ist der Wirtschaftsaufschwung an der verstärkten Rückkehr von im Ausland lebenden Bürgern erkennbar. Die große Nachfrage nach preiswertem Wohn- und Büroraum hat viele private Investitionen in den Bausektor gelenkt. Architektonisches Wahrzeichen ist der Fujairah Tower, und mit der an der Küste gelegenen Touristenanlage Mina Al Fajer dürfte sich das Emirat eine Nische auf dem Markt für luxuriöse Feriendomizile gesichert haben.

Wie viele dieser Projekte angesichts des gegenwärtigen wirtschaftlichen Klimas realisiert bzw. fertiggestellt werden, bleibt abzuwarten. Die Regierungsorgane der VAE haben die Pläne und Ambitionen der untereinander konkurrierenden Emirate stets respektiert und tragen so dazu bei, dass die VAE als geeintes Land wachsen und mit einheitlicher nationaler Identität auftreten können.

~ 2012 UND DANACH – ÜBER DEN TRAUM DES EWIGEN AUFSTIEGS

Mehr als drei Jahrzehnte lang trieben Erdöl und globales Finanzkapital die wirtschaftliche Entwicklung der VAE an. 2008 traf die internationale Bankenkrise, im Zusammenspiel mit fallenden Rohölpreisen und einem Zusammenbruch des Immobilienmarkts die VAE besonders hart. Die Auswirkungen dieses Abschwungs sind auch 2011 noch daran erkennbar, dass viele große Immobilienunternehmen in Dubai und Abu Dhabi die Regierung der VAE um finanzielle Hilfe ersuchen oder mit ihren Gläubigern eine Neuverhandlung ihrer Schulden anstreben – betroffen sind davon auch staatlich kontrollierte Unternehmen. Die globale Wirtschaftskrise führte zu einer massiven Kreditverknappung, die den Immobiliensektor stark belastete und die Immobilienpreise im Nahen Osten um fast 50 % sinken ließ. Doch hohe Ölpreise, eine günstige demografische Entwicklung, der steigende Lebensstandard, die Tatsache, dass Immobilien wieder erschwinglicher geworden sind, und ein Volumen von geplanten Hochbauten im Wert von $1,35 Billionen in den Ländern des Golf-Kooperationsrates werden die Objektentwicklung im kommenden Jahrzehnt vorantreiben. Es wird erwartet, dass die Wirtschaft der VAE in den nächsten zwei Jahren mit einer jährlichen Rate von 3 bis 4 % wächst, eine Prognose, die von stabilen Ölpreisen ausgeht und von einer robusten Entwicklung in nicht-erdölbasierten Sparten wie Bau, Infrastruktur, Finanzdienstleistungen und Immobilien. Angeführt von den Großprojekten zum Bau von Atomkraftwerken und eines emiratischen Eisenbahnnetzes, beginnen in diesem Jahr Arbeiten an Infrastrukturprojekten im Umfang von $29 Milliarden, die dem Bausektor und seinen angegliederten Industrien zahlreiche Aufträge bescheren werden. Die Regierung von Abu Dhabi hat Aufträge in Höhe von mehr als $20 Milliarden an einen südkoreanischen Konzern zum Bau von Atomkraftwerken vergeben und wird weitere $11 Milliarden für das Schienennetz der emiratischen Eisenbahnen ausgeben. Diese umfangreichen Investitionen werden die Expansions- und Diversifizierungsentwicklung der emiratischen Wirtschaft zweifellos

2007

2008

vorantreiben und auch dem Immobiliensektor starken Auftrieb verleihen. Innovationen in der Baubranche erfordern durchsetzungsfähige Experten, die bereit sind, neue Bautechniken und Anwendungskonzepte, neue Materialien, modernste Montagesysteme, Spundwand- und Fundamenttechniken zum Einsatz zu bringen. Im Zusammenspiel mit talentierten Fachleuten und einer offenen Gesellschaft wird ein kreatives Baumanagement das Land aufblühen lassen. Objektentwickler, Bauunternehmer und Architekten waren in den VAE gezwungen, eine Kultur der Innovation zu entwickeln – zunächst um einen wettbewerbsintensiven Markt zu schaffen, dann um auf diesem Markt selbst konkurrenzfähig zu bleiben. Das Ergebnis waren Entwicklungs- und Konstruktionsgroßtaten, die bis heute unerreicht sind – darunter der hexagonale, abgestützte Kern im Tragsystem des Burj Khalifa, die Entwicklung von Betonmischungen und -aushärtungsverfahren, die dem extremen, vom Gewicht des Gebäudes ausgeübten Druck standhielten und sich zugleich schnell genug in die enorme Höhe des Turms transportieren ließen, ferner die Logistik und Geschwindigkeit, mit der 210.000.000 m³ Fels, Sand und Kalkstein zur Errichtung des Palm Jumeirah Island aufgeschüttet wurden. Seit über zehn Jahren inspiriert diese kleine arabische Nation nicht nur die benachbarten Emirate, sondern auch die restliche Welt mit ihren visionären, alle Grenzen transzendierenden Projekten und einem Städtebau, der neue Superlative möglich gemacht hat, die zukünftige Generationen auf lange Sicht beeinflussen werden.

[Behr Champana Gagneron]

2010

UNITED ARAB EMIRATES IN NUMBERS

Border countries:	Oman: 410 km, Saudi Arabia: 457 km
Land boundaries:	867 km
Coastline:	1,318 km
Elevation extremes:	Arabian Gulf: 0 m
	Jabal Yibir: 1,527 m
Foundation year:	1971
UNO-Membership:	1971
Political system:	Constitutional Federation of seven Emirates: Abu Dhabi, Dubai, Sharjah, Ajman, Umm Al Quwain, Fujairah, Ras Al Khaimah
Capital:	Abu Dhabi
Total area:	83,600 km^2 (including islands)
Total population:	7,900,000 (2011 est.)
Populatioin density:	94 /km^2 (2011 est.)
Population projection 2025:	9,900,000 (2011)
Population projection 2050:	12,200,000 (2011)
Nationals:	11.47%
Non-nationals:	88.53%
Average age:	30.1 years
Average life expectancy:	75.6 years
Land use:	arable land: 0.77%, permanent crops: 2.27%, other: 96.96%
GDP – real growth rate:	3.2% (2010 est.)
GDP – per capita:	$49.600 (2010 est.)
GDP – composition by sector:	agriculture: 0.9%, industry: 53%, services: 46.1% (2010 est.)
Labour force:	3.9 million
By occupation:	agriculture: 7%, industry: 15%, services: 78%
Unemployment rate:	3.5% (2006)
Below poverty line:	19.5% (2003)
Inflation rate:	4% (2011 forecast)
Investment (gross fixed):	22.3% of GDP (2010 est.)
Industries:	Petroleum and petrochemicals, fishing, aluminium, cement, fertilisers, commercial ship repair, construction materials, some boat building, handicrafts, textiles

Oil production:	2.8 million barrel/day (2006)
Oil consumption:	435,000 barrel/day (2009)
Oil exports:	2.7 million barrel/day (2007)
Oil-proved reserves:	97.8 billion barrel (2010 est.)
Exports-commodities:	Crude oil 45%, natural gas reexports, dried fish
Export total for 2010:	$235 bn (2% of total world merchandise exports)
Import total for 2010:	$170 bn (1.4% of total world merchandise imports)

ABU DHABI	Total area: 73,000 km^2
	Population: 1,399,484 (2005 census) – City of Abu Dhabi: approx. 900,000
DUBAI	Total area: 3,900 km^2
	Population: 1,321,453 (2005 census) – 1,929,110 (2011 est.)
SHARJAH	Total area: 2,600 km^2
	Population: 793,573 (2005 census)
AJMAN	Total area: 259 km^2
	Population: 206,997 (2005 census)
UMM AL QUWAIN	Total area: 777 km^2
	Population: 49,159 (2005 census)
RAS AL KHAIMAH	Total area: 1,700 km^2
	Population: 210,063 (2005 census)
FUJAIRAH	Total area: 1,300 km^2
	Population: 125,698 (2005 census)

VEREINIGTE ARABISCHE EMIRATE IN ZAHLEN

Angrenzende Länder:	Oman: 410 km, Saudi-Arabien: 457 km
Landesgrenzen:	867 km
Küstenlinie:	1.318 km
Höhenlagen:	Persischer Golf: 0 m
	Dschabal Yibir: 1.527 m
Gründungsjahr:	1971
UNO-Mitgliedschaft:	1971
Politisches System:	Föderaler Bundesstaat von sieben Emiraten:
	Abu Dhabi, Dubai, Sharja, Ajman, Umm
	al-Kawain, Fujaira, Ras al-Khaima
Hauptstadt:	Abu Dhabi
Gesamtfläche:	83.600 km^2 (die Inseln eingeschlossen)
Gesamtbevölkerung:	7.900.000 (2011 geschätzt)
Bevölkerungsdichte:	94 / km^2 (2011 geschätzt)
Bevölkerungsprognose 2025:	9.900.000 (2011)
Bevölkerungsprognose 2050:	12.200.000 (2011)
Einheimische:	11,47 %
Ausländer:	88,53 %
Durchschnittsalter:	30,1 years
Lebenserwartung:	75,6 years
Bodennutzung:	Ackerland: 0,77 %, Dauerkulturen: 2,27 %,
	andere: 96,96 %
BIP – reale Wachstumsrate:	3,2 % (2010 geschätzt)
BIP – pro Kopf:	$ 49,600 (2010 geschätzt)
BIP – nach Bereichen:	Landwirtschaft: 0,9 %, Industrie: 53 %,
	Dienstleistungsgewerbe: 46,1%
	(2010 geschätzt)
Erwerbstätige:	3,9 Mio.
Nach Branchen:	Landwirtschaft: 7 %, Industrie: 15 %,
	Dienstleistungsgewerbe: 78 %
Arbeitslosenquote:	3,5 % (2006)
Unterhalb der Armutsgrenze:	19,5 % (2003)
Inflationsrate:	4 % (Prognose für 2011)
Bruttoanlageinvestition:	22,3 % des BIP (2010 geschätzt)
Wirtschaftsbranchen:	Erdöl und Erdölchemikalien, Fischerei,
	Aluminium, Beton, Düngemittel, Schiffs-
	reparaturen, Baumaterialien, Bootsbau,
	Handwerk, Textilindustrie

Erdölproduktion:	2,8 Mio. Barrel/Tag (2006)
Erdölverbrauch:	435.000 Barrel/Tag (2009)
Erdölexport:	2,7 Mio. Barrel/Tag (2007)
Gesicherte Erdölreserven:	97,8 Bil. Barrel (2010 geschätzt)
Exportgüter:	Rohöl 45 %, Wiederausfuhr von Erdgas,
	Trockenfisch
Exportumsatz 2010:	$ 235 Bil.
	(2 % des Welthandelsexports)
Importumsatz 2010:	$ 170 Bil.
	(1,4 % des Welthandelsimports)

ABU DHABI	Gesamtfläche: 73.000 km^2
	Bevölkerung: 1.399.484 (Zensus 2005) –
	Abu Dhabi Stadt: ca. 900.000
DUBAI	Gesamtfläche: 3.900 km^2
	Bevölkerung: 1.321.453 (Zensus 2005) –
	1.929.110 (2011 geschätzt)
SHARJA	Gesamtfläche: 2.600 km^2
	Bevölkerung: 793.573 (Zensus 2005)
AJMAN	Gesamtfläche: 259 km^2
	Bevölkerung: 206.997 (Zensus 2005)
UMM AL-KAWAIN	Gesamtfläche: 777 km^2
	Bevölkerung: 49.159 (Zensus 2005)
RAS AL-KHAIMA	Gesamtfläche: 1.700 km^2
	Bevölkerung: 210.063 (Zensus 2005)
FUJAIRA	Gesamtfläche: 1.300 km^2
	Bevölkerung: 125.698 (Zensus 2005)

Abu Dhabi

AEDAS

Boulevard Plaza / Dubai
Dubai Metro / Dubai
Empire Tower / Abu Dhabi
Pentominium / Dubai
U-Bora Towers / Dubai

designed by Andrew Bromberg

~ Aedas is an award-winning international architecture practice renowned for developing innovative and environmentally responsible solutions. The West Kowloon Terminus in Hong Kong and the Star Performance Venue in Singapore typically exemplify Aedas' contribution to the built environment. With key design centres in London, New York and Hong Kong, Aedas operates from 40 offices worldwide. This gives clients the benefit of a locally based, personal service, backed up with a global network of skills and resources. The firm works across a broad spectrum of sectors including civic and cultural, sports and leisure, commercial and residential, education, healthcare, and retail and transport, offering design expertise in architecture, masterplanning, urban design and landscape, interior design, product design and building consultancy.

~ Aedas ist ein mit vielen Preisen ausgezeichnetes internationales Architekturbüro, das sich einen Namen mit innovativen und umweltfreundlichen Lösungen gemacht hat. West Kowloon Terminus in Hongkong und Star Performance Venue in Singapur stehen beispielhaft für den Beitrag von Aedas zum Baugeschehen. Die Entwürfe entstehen weltweit in 40 Niederlassungen in London, New York und Hongkong. Damit genießen die Bauherren den Vorteil, vor Ort persönlich betreut zu werden und gleichzeitig auf ein globales Expertennetzwerk zurückgreifen zu können. Das Spektrum der Planungsleistungen des Büros ist sehr breit und umfasst öffentliche Bauten, Kultureinrichtungen, Sport- und Freizeitstätten, Gewerbe- und Wohnbauten, Bildungseinrichtungen, Bauten für den Gesundheitsbereich, Handel und Transport. Geprägt sind alle Entwürfe von fundierten Kenntnissen im Bereich Architektur, Stadt- und Landschaftsplanung, Innenarchitektur, Produktdesign und Bauberatung.

~ BOULEVARD PLAZA
Client: Emaar Properties
Site Area: 17,200 m²
Floor Area: 60,927 m²
Height: 173 m
Under construction

Boulevard Plaza stands at the gateway of the Burj Khalifa development. The importance of the site is further accentuated by being directly across the street from the Burj Khalifa Tower. The design therefore strives to suit this pioneering development. The relationship of the forms and their articulation derive from both its contextual response and as a symbol representing contemporary Islamic architecture – set within the most modern Islamic city in the world. Both towers point towards the main entrance, to greet visitors. As one moves into the area, the towers rotate their orientation as a gesture of respect to the lofty neighbour across the street. The buildings are clothed with an articulated skin recalling the veils and layers of traditional Islamic dress. The contemporary Islamic façade patterns offer symbolic context while also acting as a sunscreen, thereby significantly reducing heat loads and energy consumption. As the forms rise, they curve inwards, forming two deep, shadowed arches up into the sky – toward the crown of the Burj Khalifa.

Boulevard Plaza bildet das Tor zum neuen Areal um den Burj Khalifa und liegt dem imposanten Turm direkt gegenüber. Die Gestaltung orientiert sich daher an diesem wegweisenden Gebäude. Das Verhältnis von Form und Ausdruck ist somit einerseits vom räumlichen Kontext der Gebäude bestimmt; andererseits steht es als ein Symbol für die zeitgenössische islamische Architektur, die in der modernsten islamischen Stadt der Welt steht. Beide Türme weisen zur Begrüßung der Besucher auf den Haupt-eingangsbereich. Geht man weiter, wechseln die Türme ihre Ausrichtung – als Bekundung ihres Respekts gegenüber dem hoch aufragenden Nachbarn. Die äußere Hülle der Türme erinnert an traditionelle islamische Schleier und Gewänder. Die zeitgenössischen islamischen Fassadenmuster schaffen einen symbolischen Kontext und sind zugleich Sonnenschutz, der die Aufheizung und den Energieverbrauch reduziert. Mit zunehmender Höhe neigen sich die Außenkanten nach innen, bilden zum Himmel hin zwei tiefe, schattenspendende Bögen und verweisen auf die Krone des Burj Khalifa.

~ DUBAI METRO
Lines: 70 km
Stations: 45
Two lines under construction, two more under planning
Key metro stations equipped with taxi stations and park-and-ride facilities

A rapidly growing population and severe traffic congestion necessitated the construction of an urban rail system to provide much-needed public transport to alleviate dependence on the car, while also providing infrastructure for new commercial and residential developments. The Dubai Metro is the most advanced automated transit project in the world. The five-car trains, consisting of five compartments and three classes, provide seating for 400 passengers, plus additional standing room. The train interiors' design draws on the themes of water and air. The metro stations' sculptural shell design reflects Dubai's identity and character – strikingly modern, with a cultural reference to the country's pearl-diving heritage which brought early prosperity and is an integral part of Dubai's history. The shell structure was also conceived for functional reasons; the sweep of the smooth inner shell serves to avoid the visual complexity and somewhat industrial appearance of exposed steel truss solutions commonly used in elevated metro stations. It also remains an efficient means of creating a long span, large volume space without internal columns or supporting structures. Moreover, the curved double skin cladding provides an environmentally friendly means of cooling the roof, using traditional solar-assisted natural ventilation techniques.

Rasch wachsende Bevölkerungszahlen und viele Staus machten den Bau einer Stadtbahn notwendig; das dringend benötigte öffentliche Personennahverkehrssystem soll die Abhängigkeit vom Auto reduzieren und zugleich die notwendige Infrastruktur für neue Gewerbe- und Wohngebiete schaffen. Dubai Metro ist die modernste fahrerlose U-Bahn der Welt. Züge mit fünf Wagons zu je fünf Abteilen und drei Klassen bieten Sitzplätze für 400 Fahrgäste sowie zusätzliche Stehplätze. Die äußere, muschelartige Gestaltung der Metrostationen steht für die Identität und den Charakter Dubais – sehr modern, mit kulturellen Bezügen zu der alten Tradition des Perlentauchens, durch die das Land früh zu Reichtum kam und ein integraler Bestandteil seiner Geschichte ist. Die Schalenstruktur wurde aber auch aus praktischen Gründen gewählt: statt der Stahlträger, die in der Regel das Bild von U-Bahnstationen beherrschen und ihnen ein visuell komplexes, gleichsam industriell wirkendes Aussehen verleihen, wirkt die geschwungene Schale innen glatt und angenehm. Sie bietet auch die Möglichkeit, große, weite Räume ohne Zwischenträger oder Stützen zu überspannen. Darüber hinaus ist die gekrümmte zweischalige Verkleidung eine umweltfreundliche Methode, das Dach mit Hilfe von traditionellen, die Sonnenenergie nutzenden Lüftungstechniken zu kühlen.

~ EMPIRE TOWER
Storeys: 60
Height: 231 m
Gross Floor Area: 95,411 m²
Site Area: 7,013 m²
Ongoing

The Empire Tower is a luxury residential development located on a prime site close to Dubai's coastline, surrounded by three major streets. The complex is oriented to maximise the ocean view to the northeast and overlooks a park to the southwest. The building form is divided into a series of linear vertical blades, externally clad with a curtain wall containing thermally sufficient insulated glass units. The colour and reflectivity of the glass were chosen to make the tower stand out in its vicinity. Its curvaceous form is a direct response to its surroundings, while maximising its street presence. The building bends away from the street, the splayed vertical layers converging while rising up, before bending forward towards the sky, maximising views between the community park and the sea one block away.

Der Empire Tower, ein Wohngebäude mit Luxusapartments, steht auf einem der exklusivsten Grundstücke an der Küste Dubais und ist von drei Hauptstraßen umschlossen. Die Ausrichtung des Gebäudekomplexes nach Nordosten bietet bestmögliche Blicke auf das Meer und nach Südwesten auf einen Park. Die Gebäudeform bestimmen mehrere geradlinige, senkrechte Scheiben, die mit einer Vorhangfassade aus Isolierglaselementen verkleidet sind. Deren Farbe und Spiegeleffekt setzen den Turm bewusst von seiner Umgebung ab. Die geschwungene Form ist eine unmittelbare Reaktion auf die Umgebung und gewährleistet ein Maximum an Präsenz zur Straße hin. Das Gebäude beugt sich weg von der Straße, die unten weit gespreizten vertikalen Schichten rücken auf ihrem Weg nach oben zusammen und neigen sich dann leicht nach vorn, so dass sich vielfältigste Bezüge zum Park und zum Meer hin ergeben.

~ PENTOMINIUM
Client: Trident International Holdings
Gross Floor Area: 121,275 m^2
Total Built-up Area of the Development: 163,720 m^2
Height: 518 m
Storeys: 122
Under construction

The Pentominium tower in Dubai Marina will potentially be the tallest residential tower in the world. Named to highlight the fact that the building consists solely of penthouses, the tower had two particular challenges, due to conditions of the site: the density/proximity of its neighbouring buildings and the extreme environmental pressures of Dubai. The building design consequently has two different sides that centre around a shared core. One side is a simple extrusion that reaches the full height of the tower, which is primarily south-oriented with a system of balconies and a vertical layer of glass to mitigate solar gain. As the building rises, the glass layer becomes wider to function as a windbreak, helping to protect the balcony from the higher-velocity winds one experiences at the extreme heights of the tower. The other side of the building is a staggered shape, alternating between apartments and sky-garden voids. This is achieved with six five-storey high pods that cling structurally to the core. This alternation allows for communal or semi-private spaces and enables the tower to "breathe" within its dense context. The result is a slim, lightweight tower with a curtain wall of glass, stainless steel, aluminium and stone that sits lightly in its setting of extruded neighbours yet powerfully maintains its presence within this contrasting location.

Der Pentominium Tower in Dubai Marina wird der höchste Wohnturm der Welt werden. Mit dem Namen soll betont werden, dass das Gebäude nur aus Penthauswohnungen besteht. Die Planung des Turms musste sich zwei Herausforderungen stellen: der Nähe zu den Nachbargebäuden und den Umweltbelastungen in Dubai. Daher besitzt das Gebäude zwei unterschiedliche Seiten, die sich um einen gemeinsamen Gebäudekern legen. Eine Seite steigt glatt bis zum höchsten Punkt des Turmes auf; sie ist hauptsächlich nach Süden ausgerichtet, besitzt Balkone und ist mit Glas verkleidet, was die Aufheizung reduziert. Im oberen Bereich dient die Glasfront auch als Windschutz für die Balkone, die in dieser extremen Höhe starken Winden ausgesetzt sind. Auf der anderen Seite sind Wohnungen und Sky-Garden-Bereiche über fünf Geschosse im Wechsel angeordnet und am Gebäudekern verankert. Durch diese alternierende Anordnung entstehen gemeinschaftlich nutzbare beziehungsweise halböffentliche Räume und das Gebäude kann trotz seiner hohen Dichte „atmen". Das Ergebnis ist ein schlanker, leichter Turm mit einer Vorhangfassade aus Glas, Edelstahl, Aluminium und Naturstein, der zwanglos seinen Platz zwischen den Nachbargebäuden einnimmt und doch kraftvoll seine Präsenz innerhalb eines Standortes voller Gegensätze behauptet.

~ U-BORA TOWERS
Client: Bando Engineering & Construction Co. Ltd
Gross Floor Area: 119,298 m²
Ongoing

The U-Bora Tower complex is a mixed-use development situated in the heart of Dubai's Business Bay district. The design gives equal attention to its office, residential and podium use – in order to maximise opportunities and viabilities within the site's context. The structure's floors appear to progressively twist and turn, with the contours bulging outwards as the tower ascends into the sky. The office-tower position is rotated from the orthogonal at street level to help focus the office space down future view corridors, past surrounding developments towards the sea. As the tower increases in height, its four faces respond directly to their three-dimensional context; all twisting at varying degrees and angles to re-orient their faces to maximise views. The residential block does not compete with the surrounding towers in height. Instead, it remains low and focused to the adjacent water body to the south. By designing the block as a linear bar rising from twelve floors at the tower end to 15 floors at the western end, a significantly greater percentage of units get an uninterrupted sea view. All three components are bound together with a 10,000 m² landscaped public deck that is accessible from all three sides of the scheme. The architecture is powerful, pure and dynamic, with the aim of becoming a focal development in a setting of competing attention. Unique to its setting in Business Bay, this project is set to become a model development in the Middle East.

U-Bora Towers ist ein Gebäudekomplex mit unterschiedlichen Nutzungen im Zentrum des Business Bay District von Dubai. Die Gestaltung berücksichtigt in gleicher Weise die unterschiedlichen Erfordernisse, die mit der Nutzung als Büro- und Wohnräume sowie diejenigen im Bereich des Gebäudesockels einhergehen, um die verschiedenen Möglichkeiten des Standorts zu optimieren. Die Geschosse des Büroturms schrauben sich förmlich nach oben, die Außenkanten wölben sich mit zunehmender Höhe nach außen. Der gesamte Turm wird aus der rechteckigen Form auf Straßenniveau herausgedreht, um in den Büroräumen zukünftig Blickachsen vorbei an neu entstehenden Gebäuden auf das Meer zu ermöglichen. Mit zunehmender Höhe gehen die vier Turmseiten stärker auf den dreidimensionalen Kontext ein; sie alle sind in unterschiedlicher Stärke und jeweils eigenem Winkel gedreht, um einen bestmöglichen Blick zu bieten. Der Wohnblock ragt nicht so weit in die Höhe wie die Türme der Umgebung. Stattdessen bleibt er niedrig und legt seinen Fokus auf die angrenzende Wasserfläche im Süden. Indem der Block als geradliniger Riegel mit 12 Turmgeschossen und 15 Etagen am westlichen Ende geplant ist, erhalten mehr Wohneinheiten einen direkten Blick auf das Meer. Alle drei Gebäudeteile sind durch eine 10.000 m² große öffentliche Gartenanlage verbunden, die von allen drei Seiten zugänglich ist. Die Architektur ist kraftvoll, rein und dynamisch; es soll ein Zentrum innerhalb eines Bereichs entstehen, in dem viele Bauten um Aufmerksamkeit buhlen. Die Lage innerhalb des Business Bay District ist einmalig, und das Projekt wird sicherlich Modellcharakter für den Nahen Osten haben.

ARCHGROUP CONSULTANTS

Emirates Park Towers Hotel / Dubai

~ The process of unifying form and function involves perseverance, analytical problem-solving and creativity. For Archgroup, this also means an architecture that is not constrained by an individual or particular style. The practice has designed a range of buildings – from the Italian Renaissance-style Westin Hotel to the art deco-inspired Oasis Shopping Mall; contemporary designs for the Emirates Park Tower and Grosvenor House hotels, to indigenous Arabic architectural forms for the Khasab Hotel in Oman and the palatial Rajasthani style for the Taj Exotica Resort & Spa on Dubai's Palm Island. With this approach, Archgroup encourages alternative forms of expression, with a commitment to innovation and quality.

~ Die Zusammenführung von Form und Funktion braucht Beharrlichkeit, die Fähigkeit zu analytischer Problemlösung und Kreativität. Für Archgroup bedeutet das auch eine Architektur, die nicht auf einen individuellen oder bestimmten Stil beschränkt ist. Das Büro entwarf bereits viele unterschiedliche Gebäude – vom Westin Hotel im Stil der italienischen Renaissance bis zur Oasis Shopping Mall in einem an das Art déco angelehnten Stil, von zeitgenössischen Gestaltungen für die Emirats Park Towers und die Grosvenor House Hotels bis zu traditionellen arabischen Bauformen für das Khasab Hotel in Oman und dem prunkvollen rajasthanischen Stil für das Taj Exotica Resort & Spa auf der Palmeninsel von Dubai. Mit diesem Ansatz ermöglicht Archgroup innovative und qualitätvolle alternative Ausdrucksformen.

~ EMIRATES PARK TOWERS HOTEL
Storeys: 88
Height: 355 m
Built-up Area: 330,770 m²
Completion date of first tower: march 2012

The form of the 70-storey twin towers located in the Business Bay development was inspired by the date palm – a symbol deeply entrenched in Arabic culture. This flagship project for the hotel division of Emirates Airline comprises 1,368 guest rooms, 240 suites, 9 retail outlets, 17 restaurants and one of the largest spas in Dubai. A podium houses the public areas and landscaped terrace. The exterior detailing belies the sophisticated engineering and technological input within the towers. The structure is supported by a 3.9 m thick raft on 1.2 m diameter piles. The hotel tower has a central, oval-shaped core with internal lift core walls providing lateral stability. At typical floor level, shear walls float from 2.4 x 5.2 m deep beams at transfer level. To ensure lateral stability of the structure and reduce wind accelerations at roof level, reinforced concrete outriggers are introduced at the 14th, 30th and 48th levels. The structural and electro-mechanical design befits a building which aspires to set the benchmark for hotels in the region.

Die Form der 70-geschossigen Zwillingstürme im Business Bay District leitet sich aus der Dattelpalme, einem tief in der arabischen Kultur verwurzelten Symbol, ab. Dieses Vorzeigeprojekt der Hotelsparte von Emirates Airline bietet Platz für 1368 Zimmer, 240 Suiten, 9 Geschäfte, 17 Restaurants und eines der größten Wellnessareale in Dubai. Der Sockelbereich ist öffentlich zugänglich und mit begrünten Terrassen angelegt. Die Außengestaltung lässt kaum die komplexen baukonstruktiven und technischen Elemente im Turminneren erahnen. Die Konstruktion steht auf einer 3,9 m dicken Fundamentplatte auf Stützen mit 1,2 m Durchmesser. Der Hotelturm besitzt in der Mitte einen ovalen Kern, dessen Aufzugswände der Seitenaussteifung dienen. Auf den Geschossebenen hängen Querwände von 2,4 x 5,2 m starken Balkenträgern der Transferebene herab. Für die Seitenaussteifung der Konstruktion und zur Verringerung der Windbeschleunigung auf der Ebene des Daches wurden Stahlbetonausleger auf der 14., 30. und 48. Etage eingebaut. Gestalterisch und technisch setzt das Gebäude einen Maßstab für die Hotelplanung der Region.

ASYMPTOTE ARCHITECTURE

The Yas Hotel / Abu Dhabi
Strata Tower / Abu Dhabi

~ Established in 1989 by Hani Rashid and Lise Anne Couture, Asymptote Architecture has been working at the forefront of technological innovation within the architectural profession. With a range of commissions around the world, the award-winning practice has won international acclaim for its visionary building projects in the US, Europe and the UAE, as well as masterplanning, art installations, exhibition and product design, and groundbreaking digital spatial environments. Asymptote's work has been widely published and is in various private and public collections.

~ Asymptote Architecture wurde 1989 von Hani Rashid und Lise Anne Couture gegründet und gehört zur Spitze der technologisch innovativ arbeitenden Architekturbüros. Das Team arbeitet weltweit an unterschiedlichen Projekten, ist mit vielen Preisen ausgezeichnet worden und findet international großen Zuspruch für die visionären Bauprojekte in den USA, Europa und in den VAE sowie für Stadtplanung, Kunstinstallationen, Ausstellungen, Produktdesign und die bahnbrechenden digitalen Raumgestaltungen. Die Arbeiten von Asymptote wurden vielfach veröffentlicht und befinden sich in privaten und öffentlichen Sammlungen.

~ THE YAS HOTEL
Client: Aldar Properties
Size: 85,000 m²
Completion: 2010

The Yas Hotel is the key architectural feature of Abu Dhabi's ambitious Yas Marina development. The world's first building designed to span a Grand Prix race circuit, Asymptote envisaged an architectural landmark embodying key influences and inspirations – from the aesthetic forms associated with speed, movement and spectacle to the artistry and geometries forming the basis of ancient Islamic art and craft traditions. Of particular architectural and engineering significance, the project's design encompasses a 217 m expanse of sweeping, curvilinear steel forms, featuring 5,800 pivoting diamond-shaped glass panels. This grid shell component affords the building an architectural "veil" inside which two hotel towers are linked by a bridge constructed as a sculpted steel object passing above the Formula 1 track as it snakes its way through the building complex. The curved exterior visually connects and fuses the entire complex while producing optical effects and reflections that play against the surrounding sky, sea and desert landscape. The architecture as a whole performs both as an environmentally responsive solution as well as an architecture of spectacle and event. The jewel-like composition responds visually and tectonically to its environment to create a distinct and powerful sense of place as well as a breathtaking backdrop to the Formula 1 race and other events that the building will host. The Yas Hotel was designed to be a landmark destination for both Abu Dhabi and the wider UAE.

Das Yas Hotel ist das Architekturhighlight des ehrgeizigen Entwicklungsprojekts der Yas Marina von Abu Dhabi und weltweit das erste Gebäude über einer Grand-Prix-Rennstrecke. Asymptote plante eine herausragende Anlage, in der sich wichtige Einflüsse und Inspirationen vereinen – von der Gestaltung, die bestimmt ist von Geschwindigkeit, Bewegung und Spektakel, bis zu Formen aus der alten islamischen Kunst und kunsthandwerklichen Traditionen. Baulich und technisch besonders bedeutend ist die 217 m lange Dachfläche mit weit spannenden, geschwungenen Stahlträgern und mit 5800 wie Diamanten geformten Glasplatten. Dieses Netz legt sich wie ein Glasschleier über die zwei Hoteltürme. Sie sind durch eine Brücke verbunden, die als dekoratives Stahlobjekt über das geschlungene Rund der Formel-1-Strecke verläuft. Die geschwungene Fassade bindet optisch den gesamten Komplex zusammen und lässt interessante visuelle Effekte und Reflexionen vor dem weiten Himmel, dem Meer und der Wüstenlandschaft entstehen. Die gesamte Architektur ist sowohl eine umweltfreundliche Lösung als auch eine bauliche Umsetzung von Spektakel und Event. Die wie ein Edelstein wirkende Komposition reagiert optisch und tektonisch auf ihr Umfeld und schafft so ein besonderes und kraftvolles Gefühl für den Ort wie auch ein atemberaubendes Ambiente für die Formel-1-Rennen und andere Veranstaltungen. Das Yas Hotel soll ein ganz besonderes Reiseziel und ein Wahrzeichen von Abu Dhabi und den gesamten VAE werden.

~ STRATA TOWER
Client: Aldar Properties PJSC
Total Size: 53,357 m^2
Ongoing

As a signature architectural statement, the Strata Tower's articulate, striking physical presence seeks to encapsulate meaning through the use of abstract form drawn from both local cultural landscapes and motifs and dynamic forces of global influence. The design uses primarily mathematical means to achieve both a poetic, as well as highly pertinent, architecture for the UAE – a country in a state of flux, with ambitions for continued rapid growth. The Strata Tower's innovative form was created using state-of-the-art parametric modelling tools and techniques from the design process to the production phase. The building's design emerged from various influences and factors – including economies of production and fabrication, with special consideration for environmental sustainability. Sophisticated computer modelling and tools were used to produce the building's intelligent, environmentally responsive louver system that is held in a unique, cantilevered structure. The exoskeleton veils the entire tower in a shimmering curvilinear form set against Abu Dhabi's surrounding desert and sea, embracing and reflecting the ever-changing light and atmospheres that enfold and contain it. As architecture, the Strata Tower resists being an overt, singular gesture reliant on a set meaning or association. Rather, the mathematical properties used, not unlike those in the manifestation of the arabesque or abstract calligraphy, give the building its supreme elegance, prominence and potential for meaning and significance.

Die abstrakte Form des Strata Tower ist von den lokalen kulturellen Traditionen ebenso inspiriert wie von den dynamischen Kräften weltweiter Einflüsse; entstehen soll hier ein weithin sichtbares Gebäude mit großer Aussagekraft und kraftvoller Präsenz. Die Gestaltung versucht mit primär mathematischen Mitteln, sowohl eine poetische als auch sehr sachliche Architektur für die VAE zu schaffen – ein Land im Wandel mit dem Ziel eines kontinuierlichen schnellen Wachstums. Durch Anwendung modernster parametrischer Modellierungstechniken ergab sich die innovative Form des Strata Tower. Die Gestaltung beeinflussten zudem verschiedene andere Faktoren, wobei solchen Produktions- und Herstellungsmethoden besondere Bedeutung zukam, bei denen Umweltfreundlichkeit und Nachhaltigkeit eine herausgehobene Rolle spielen. Mit Hilfe komplexer Computermodelle entstanden intelligente, auf die Witterung reagierende, speziell verankerte Lamellen. Das Außenskelett umhüllt den Turm mit seiner gedrehten Form inmitten von Abu Dhabis Wüste und Meer. Mit seinem Glanz taucht er ein in das sich ständig wandelnde Licht und schafft so eine immer neue Atmosphäre. Als Baukörper widersteht der Strata Tower dem Versuch, eine offensichtliche, singuläre Geste zu sein, die auf eine vorgegebene Palette von Bedeutungen oder Assoziationen vertraut. Stattdessen geben die mathematischen Eigenschaften – vergleichbar mit der verschnörkelten oder abstrakten Kalligrafie – dem Gebäude seine großartige Eleganz, Prominenz und Bedeutungsvielfalt.

ATKINS

Atrium City / Dubai
DIFC Lighthouse Tower / Dubai
X-Change Gateway / Dubai
Iris Bay / Dubai

~ Established in 1934, engineering consultancy Atkins continues to build on its engineering roots, while forging into architecture. By 1978, when it first started working in the Emirates, the UK firm had a well-developed architectural division. Today, it is one of the largest consultancies in the world and has developed high standards in every field of construction. Atkins celebrated the millennium with the creation of Dubai's iconic Burj Al Arab hotel, which played a part in consolidating Dubai's position on the world map. Atkins has since completed a wide range of projects worldwide, drawing on its in-house capabilities to produce fully integrated, efficient designs that are striking yet respectful of context.

~ Das britische Büro Atkins wurde 1934 gegründet und bietet, seiner Tradition folgend, sowohl bautechnische Beratungen als auch Bauplanungen. Bereits 1978, als die ersten Planungen in den Arabischen Emiraten begannen, gab es eine erfahrene Architekturabteilung. Heute ist Atkins eines der größten Beratungsunternehmen der Welt und übernimmt Bauleistungen auf höchstem Niveau. Zur Jahrtausendwende konnte Atkins in Dubai die Fertigstellung des bereits legendären Burj-al-Arab-Hotels feiern, das maßgeblich zur Konsolidierung von Dubais weltpolitischer Bedeutung beitrug. Seit dieser Zeit hat Atkins weltweit sehr viele Projekte fertiggestellt und vertraut dabei auf die Fähigkeiten der Mitarbeiter, effiziente Gesamtgestaltungen zu entwickeln – Projekte, die auffallen, aber dennoch ihrem Kontext mit Achtung begegnen.

~ ATRIUM CITY
Total Area: 600,000 m²
Height: 600 m
Ongoing

The site for this proposed development borders the new downtown Dubai neighbourhood and the Dubai International Financial Centre, south of the creek. It is also an important transport intersection, bringing together a major road junction, the Dubai Metro red line, a new system of abra ferries serving a series of lagoons and canals and pedestrian walkways into Garden City, a new environmentally sensitive development running parallel to the coastline. The brief called for two 700 m towers which, while shorter in terms of overall height, provide significantly more residential units than the Burj Khalifa. The towers provide substantial floor plates, which are significantly expanded in the podium to house commercial and retail spaces. The design responds to the junction between desert and sea; the airy solidity of the desert is carried across the podium in layers, and then rises into the towers in one wave, matched and balanced by the transparency and coolness of the water in a similar wave on the sea side. The resultant form provides shelter to the south elevations, views and light to cooler north, and combines the towers and podium into a single flowing form compounded with layers of opacity and solidity. The differing tower heights and the amorphous but controlled shape of the podium reflect the layered form of the sea's waves and dunes as they meet.

Das Planungsareal grenzt an das neue Innenstadtviertel von Dubai und das Dubai International Financial Centre, südlich des Flusses. Es ist auch ein bedeutender Verkehrsknotenpunkt, an dem sich mehrere Straßen kreuzen, die Metrozüge der roten Linie halten und die Boote zu den Lagunen und Kanälen des neuen Abra-Fährsystems anlegen; zudem gibt es Fußgängerwege zur Garden City, einem neuen ökologischen Entwicklungsgebiet parallel zur Küste. Im Bauprogramm waren zwei 700 m hohe Türme gefordert, in denen bei geringerer Gesamthöhe deutlich mehr Wohneinheiten untergebracht werden sollen als im Burj Khalifa. Die Türme bieten viel Raum auf den Geschossebenen, der Sockelbereich ist stark ausgeweitet, um Flächen für gewerbliche Einrichtungen und Läden zu erhalten. Die Gestaltung reagiert auf den Standort zwischen Wüste und Meer. Wie Sanddünen schichten sich die Baukörper wellenförmig zum Sockelbereich auf und vereinen sich dann in einer großen Geste zu jeweils einem hoch aufragenden Turm, in dem sich die Transparenz und Kühle des Meerwassers widerspiegeln. Die sich daraus ergebende Form schirmt die Südseite ab, bietet dem kühleren Norden Ausblick und Licht und verbindet die Türme und den Sockel zu einer einzigen fließenden Form aus opaken und massiven Schichten. In den unterschiedlichen Turmhöhen und der amorphen, aber klaren Sockelform findet sich des Wellenspiel von Meer und Wüste wieder.

~ DIFC LIGHTHOUSE TOWER
Client: Dubai International Financial Centre
Total Area: 172,600 m²
Office space: 90,000 m²
Height: 402 m
Storeys: 64
Ongoing

Lighthouses are traditionally cylindrical; however, this one is distinctly rectilinear and at a little over 400 m in height, comfortably surpasses its neighbours, to provide a landmark in Dubai's financial district – entirely appropriate, given its function as the headquarters of the body that administers this progressive location. Perhaps more importantly, The Lighthouse is guiding the way: incorporating over 50 sustainable technologies it represents a significant step forward in sustainable design. Whereas other buildings are conceived as a response to a requirement for accommodation with a few sustainable technologies subsequently applied, The Lighthouse's design adopted sustainability as a prime component of the building's brief. This approach drives the building form and orientation, its planning and massing – so being a fundamental part of the architecture. The result is a 55% reduction in electricity consumption, 36% reduction in water usage, and 49% reduction in district cooling energy, compared to the standard. Without compromises in architectural terms, the building's occupants are unlikely to notice the myriad techniques that respond to their presence. They will be unaware, for example, that as the elevator slows comfortably to a stop, it is generating power in the process. Nor that the attractive patterns on the building exterior, which represent the DIFC logo while recalling the mashrabia screen of traditional Arabian architecture, also control glare, reduce solar gain and generate electricity.

Leuchttürme sind traditionell rund, aber dieser besitzt eine eigenwillig rechteckige Form. Mit etwas über 400 m Höhe überragt er seine Nachbargebäude deutlich und ist ein Wahrzeichen in Dubais Financial District, womit er seiner Funktion als Verwaltungssitz dieses aufstrebenden Bezirks gerecht wird. The Lighthouse ist aber auch in anderer Hinsicht wegweisend, denn mit der Anwendung von über 50 Nachhaltigkeitstechnologien geht es einen bedeutenden Schritt in Richtung nachhaltige Gestaltung. Während andere Gebäude eher eine Reaktion auf die Forderung nach dem Einbau einiger nachhaltiger Techniken sind, war bei diesem Entwurf die Nachhaltigkeit ein Hauptelement des geforderten Bauprogramms. Dieser Ansatz bestimmt die Form und Ausrichtung des Gebäudes, die Planung und Massenverteilung – und ist damit ein fundamentaler Bestandteil der Architektur. Das Ergebnis ist im Vergleich zu anderen Gebäuden eine Reduktion des Stromverbrauchs um 55 %, des Wasserverbrauchs um 36 % und des Fernkältebedarfs um 49 %. Architektonisch mussten keine Kompromisse eingegangen werden und die Nutzer bemerken kaum die vielfältigen Techniken, die zum Einsatz kommen. Sie merken beispielsweise nicht, dass der Aufzug beim sanften Abbremsen vor dem Halt Strom erzeugt oder dass die attraktiven Muster der Gebäudefassade, die das DIFC-Logo darstellen und an ein Maschrabijja-Gitterfenster aus der traditionellen arabischen Architektur erinnern, auch die Blendwirkung kontrollieren, die Aufheizung reduzieren und zugleich Strom produzieren.

~ X-CHANGE GATEWAY
Total Area: 350,000 m²
Ongoing

X-Change Gateway is the response to a design challenge: to create a zero-energy "supertower", a significant milestone on the road to sustainability in architecture. The structure combines two raking towers, which intersect at midpoint to create a dynamic composition. The crossed towers are rooted in commercial reality, in that larger, more powerful clients generally prefer larger suites towards the top of a building, whereas smaller organisations prefer low-level, smaller units. In this building form, the combined tower at high level and the independent towers lower down provide the required mix. The concrete exoskeleton terminates at 350 m above ground to become a steel version rising to 500 m, visually similar but open to the atmosphere. This structural system provides clear internal spaces, desirable for office and retail spaces, where the column-free floors enable outstanding flexibility, but vital where large plant items are required. The levels above the crossing point are given over to energy generation, with the steel structure housing a number of environmentally sensitive technologies. The most significant are the six 50 m diameter wind turbines, comfortably housed in the wide, open spaces of the skeleton structure. These power the building and more; combined with PV panels to shade the south elevations, providing a generative capacity that is 33% more than required to run the X-Change Gateway. The excess allows the tower to function in low wind conditions, and provides a potential supply to surrounding developments. A comfortably self-sustaining tower form for the future.

X-Change Gateway ist die Antwort auf eine Planungsherausforderung nach einem Null-Energie-„Superturm" als wichtigem Meilenstein auf dem Weg zu Nachhaltigkeit in der Architektur. Das Gebäude besteht aus zwei geneigten Türmen, die sich in der Mitte treffen und so eine dynamische Komposition schaffen. Die gekreuzten Türme reagieren auf einen bestimmten wirtschaftlichen Bedarf: Große zahlungskräftige Kunden bevorzugen in der Regel relativ große Suiten im oberen Bereich eines Gebäudes, während kleinere Organisationen lieber unten in kleineren Einheiten untergebracht sind. Bei dieser Gebäudeform – zwei Türme oben verschmolzen und unten getrennt – entsteht der gewünschte Mix. Das Außenskelett aus Beton endet 350 m über dem Boden und wird als optisch ähnliches, aber offenes Stahlskelett bis auf 500 m Höhe fortgeführt. So entstehen offene Grundrisse und stützenfreie Geschosse mit außergewöhnlicher Flexibilität. Die Ebenen über dem Kreuzungsbereich dienen der Energieerzeugung. In der Stahlkonstruktion sind eine Reihe umweltempfindlicher Technologien eingebaut. Von besonderer Bedeutung sind die sechs Windturbinen mit einem Durchmesser von 50 m, die sich gut in die offene Skelettkonstruktion einfügen. Sie liefern diesem und anderen Gebäuden Strom. Zusammen mit den Photovoltaikelementen, die die Südfassade verschatten, erzeugen sie 33 % mehr Energie als für den Gebäudebetrieb notwendig wäre. Durch diesen Überschuss erfüllt der Turm auch bei wenig Wind die ökologischen Anforderungen und kann Gebäude der Umgebung mitversorgen – das Zukunftsmodell eines energetisch autarken Gebäudes.

~ IRIS BAY
Client: Sheth Estate Ltd
Area: 36,000 m²
Height: 170 m
Storeys: 32
Under construction
Envisioned completion: 2012

A client's desire to create a distinctive building with a readily identifiable identity opened the way for Atkins to explore sustainability issues free from the constraints of more conservative tower forms. The result is everything and more that the client sought. The building is a response to the primary requirement to reduce heat gain, allowing for a particularly efficient internal climate control system. This was achieved through unusually low window-to-wall ratios to the west and east, while the narrow north and south aspects incorporate more open glazing, with balconies and opening shade, with photovoltaic panels providing natural ventilation and a connection with the outside environment. The angling of these façades, and the para-spherical shells which clad the side elevations, modify the natural breezes and create stack-effect ventilation to achieve areas of negative and positive pressure, reducing the need for powered ventilation and cooling systems. The building is located in Dubai's Business Bay, notable for some of the most distinctive new buildings in a city already fêted for its avant-garde architecture. While not yet complete, Iris Bay has fast become a landmark structure, as foreseen by the client.

Der Wunsch des Bauherren, ein besonderes Gebäude mit einer klar erkennbaren Identität zu schaffen, gab Atkins die Möglichkeit, das Thema Nachhaltigkeit frei von den Zwängen eher konservativer Turmformen anzugehen. Das Ergebnis übertraf die Erwartungen des Bauherren bei weitem. Das Gebäude ist eine Antwort auf die wichtigste Anforderung, eine möglichst geringe Aufheizung durch die Sonne, was den Einbau eines besonders effizienten Systems zur Regulierung des Innenraumklimas ermöglicht. So gibt es im Westen und Osten im Vergleich zur Wandfläche verhältnismäßig wenig Fenster; die schmalen Nord- und Südseiten sind dagegen Glasflächen mit Balkonen und zu öffnenden Verschattungselementen sowie Photovoltaikpaneele mit Belüftungsfunktion und Verbindung nach draußen. Die Krümmung der Fassaden und die halbrunden Schalen, die die seitlichen Fassaden verkleiden, beeinflussen die Luftströme und erzeugen einen Kamineffekt, durch den Bereiche mit Über- beziehungsweise Unterdruck entstehen, wodurch weniger strombetriebene Belüftung und Kühlung notwendig ist. Das Gebäude steht in Dubais Business Bay District, wo sich einige der bemerkenswertesten neuen Gebäude einer Stadt befinden, die für ihre avantgardistische Architektur gefeiert wird.

DBI DESIGN

Etihad Towers / Abu Dhabi

~ Based in Brisbane, Australia, DBI is a multidisciplinary design practice whose output spans architecture, interior and landscape design and masterplanning. With a 70-strong team, the firm's portfolio features major resorts, hotels and commercial projects in China, Taiwan, Indonesia, Malaysia and the Philippines. DBI's most recent project, The Wave at Broadbeach, Australia, was recently awarded second prize in the Worldwide Emporis design awards.

~ Das im australischen Brisbane angesiedelte interdisziplinäre Büro arbeitet in den Bereichen Architektur, Innenarchitektur, Landschaftsarchitektur und Stadtplanung. Ein 70-köpfiges Team plant große Anlagen, Hotels und gewerbliche Projekte in China, Taiwan, Indonesien, Malaysia und auf den Philippinen. Das jüngste Projekt von DBI, The Wave im australischem Broadbeach, wurde kürzlich mit dem zweiten Preis bei den Worldwide Emporis Design Awards ausgezeichnet.

~ ETIHAD TOWERS

5 towers (tallest: 300 m)

3 residential apartment towers, 1 office tower,
and 1 hotel/serviced apartment tower

Storeys: 55–77

Total Built-up Area: 500,000 m^2

46,000 m^2 lettable office area

885 residential apartments in a variety of configurations, retail centre

2,500 m^2 ballroom and convention centre – the largest in Abu Dhabi

5 star hotel, 199 serviced apartments, 12 restaurants

380,000 m^3 of concrete

65,000 t of steel

135,000 m^2 of tower curtain walling

6,000 m^2 of structural glazing within the podium

850,000 m^2 of plaster

Under construction, project opening: late 2011

The Etihad Towers development is located on a multi-level podium, facing a prominent waterfront site, close to Abu Dhabi's business district, opposite the Emirates Palace Hotel. The project was conceived as an architectural structure with the potential to become an emblem of Abu Dhabi. Throughout history, architecture has been used to symbolise nations' religious, cultural, political and economic aspirations and successes. With its sculptural forms, Etihad Towers is intended to symbolise the UAE capital as a progressive and technologically sophisticated city of great prestige, culture and economic wealth. The building's formal composition is intended to be a sculptural composition of dramatic forms – providing great visual drama. The tower surfaces are monolithic and, unlike conventional building fenestration, which is composed of windows, walls and floor slabs, the structures will read as a towering urban sculpture, devoid of the obvious signifiers of scale of occupation, such as window openings. The building will effectively appear scaleless and enigmatic. Its design draws on a number of references, fused into a coherent construct. These multiple precursors allow for multiple readings of the final building: from different directions the complex could be referring to a billowing sail, a fleet of vessels, a traditional sword and a pearl shell. Such diverse references and forms are drawn together in a composition which can be seen as an allusion to the unity of the UAE – and a singularly architectural statement for its capital city.

Die Etihad Towers erheben sich über einem mehrgeschossigen Sockel. Das Areal an der Küste grenzt an Abu Dhabis Geschäftsviertel und befindet sich gegenüber vom Empirates Palace Hotel. Mit den Etihad Towers soll ein Gebäudekomplex mit Symbolkraft für Abu Dhabi entstehen. Schon immer wurde Architektur genutzt, um die Ziele und Erfolge in den Bereichen Religion, Kultur, Politik und Wirtschaft eines Landes zu symbolisieren. Mit ihren prägnanten Formen stellen die Etihad Towers die Hauptstadt der VAE als eine fortschrittliche und technologisch innovative Stadt mit großem Ansehen, viel Kultur und wirtschaftlichem Reichtum dar. Die einzelnen Gebäude sind eine Komposition dramatischer Formen, die Oberflächen sind monolithisch und besitzen nicht die konventionelle Fassadenstruktur aus Fenstern, Wänden und Decken. Stattdessen gleichen die Türme eher hoch aufragenden urbanen Skulpturen, ohne die üblichen Hinweise auf eine Nutzung, wie sie beispielsweise Fensteröffnungen liefern. Das Gebäude wird sich jedem Vergleich entziehen und geheimnisvoll wirken. In der Gestaltung gibt es vielfältige architektonische Bezüge, die zu einem kohärenten Ganzen verschmelzen. Diese Anklänge ermöglichen verschiedene Lesarten für das endgültige Gebäude: je nach Richtung, aus der man die Gebäude sieht, denkt man an ein vom Wind geblähtes Segel, an Boote, an ein traditionelles Schwert oder an eine Perlmuschel. Die unterschiedlichen Bezüge und Formen werden zu einer Komposition zusammengefasst, die auch auf die Einheit der VAE anspielen – eine einzigartige architektonische Geste für deren Hauptstadt.

DXB-LAB

Code Business Tower / Dubai

~ dxb-lab is an award-winning architecture practice based in Dubai, established in 2000 by Khalid Al Najjar and Shahab Lutfi. After studying in Europe and the US, the Emirati partners have succeeded in establishing a local firm with a distinguished reputation across the Middle East. Through an applied combination of design principles, architectural innovation and modern technologies, dxb-lab relishes its Arabic roots and respects local customs and traditions in the built environment. Projects range from private residences, commercial and office buildings to cultural and public projects, hotel resorts and masterplans.

~ dxb-lab ist ein in Dubai angesiedeltes Architekturbüro, das im Jahr 2000 von Khalid Al Najjar und Shahab Lutfi gegründet und bereits mit mehreren Preisen ausgezeichnet wurde. Nach ihrem Studium in Europa und den USA gelang es den beiden Partnern, vor Ort ein Büro aufzubauen, das im Nahen Osten großes Ansehen genießt. Durch eine besondere Kombination von Gestaltungsprinzipien, innovativer Architektur und modernen Technologien bringt dxb-lab seine arabischen Wurzeln ein und achtet die örtlichen Bräuche und Traditionen im gebauten Umfeld. Die Projekte reichen von privaten Wohnhäusern über Gewerbe- und Bürobauten bis zu kulturellen und öffentlichen Projekten, Hotelanlagen und städtebaulichen Masterplänen.

~ CODE BUSINESS TOWER
2010 Middle East Architect Award – Best Commercial Building of the Year
Storeys: 14
Completed: 2010

The black and white Code Tower makes a distinctive contribution to a city saturated with high-rises that try to be different yet conversely look the same. Such a metropolitan condition deserves a different contribution to a new city like Dubai, which seeks to define its new character through its skyline. A solemn and indifferent building with plenty of style and aura. This tower does not try to imitate its otherwise chaotic surroundings; rather, it's as though the city is inspired by its presence. Open plan without columns, the floor weight is carried to the ground by the two side load-bearing walls, which define the tower's rising form. Cutout patterns on the façade give the tower an abstract statement in a predominantly figurative city. The elevations are organised like a plan. The same two-dimensional planes also become a ceiling for the entrance lobby that floats over the exposed concrete lobby floor. A glass façade defines the third elevation of the building. The black granite exterior on the fourth façade and its direct expression in the interior effectively turns the building inside out. The core of the tower is also dressed in black granite. A black hole and a public space – this is where the public vertical circulation is gathered. Visiting the building is an experience of linear perspectives and extended visual lines out towards the sky and horizon. This structure is a coordinated geometry that ties spaces and materials together. A grid-inspired building, the endlessness is reflected by the long corridors for some of the tower's offices; passages of space and movement. The panels are customised with visible joints to give a special scale and make the geometric visual visible at all times. This project has created a new paradigm of 21st-century architecture for Dubai – localised, but minus any applied theme and of a scale that feels more like a neighbourhood urban building than an anonymous, generic city tower.

[George Katodrytis]

Der schwarz-weiße Code Tower bringt sich erfrischend anders in eine Stadt ein, in deren Silhouette es bereits viele Wolkenkratzer gibt, die alle anders sein wollen, aber in gewisser Weise doch alle gleich aussehen. Um solche Uniformität zu vermeiden – zumal in einer neuen Stadt wie Dubai, die versucht, ihren Charakter über die Skyline zu definieren – bedarf es eines ganz eigenen Beitrags. Dementsprechend ist der Code Tower ein ernstes und stilles Gebäude mit Stil und Aura. Dieser Turm versucht nicht, sein eher chaotisches Umfeld zu imitieren; vielmehr wirkt die Stadt durch seine Präsenz inspiriert. Die Grundrisse sind offen und stützenfrei, das Gewicht der Decken ruht auf den beiden tragenden Seitenwänden, die die hoch aufragende Form des Turms definieren. Die ausgeschnittenen Elemente geben der Fassade eine abstrakte Wirkung in einer Stadt mit eher figurativen Gestaltungsmustern. Die Ansichten sind zweidimensional als Ebenen gestaltet, und diese Ebenen werden zur Decke in der Eingangshalle, die über dem Sichtbetonboden der Halle schwebt. Eine Glasfassade bildet die dritte Ansicht des Gebäudes. Der schwarze Granit der vierten Fassade und dessen Entsprechung im Inneren wenden wirkungsvoll das Innere nach außen. Der innere Kern des Turmes ist ebenfalls mit schwarzem Granit verkleidet. Ein schwarzes Loch und ein öffentlicher Raum – hier sind die vertikalen Zugangsmöglichkeiten zusammengefasst. Das Gebäude setzt auf das Erleben linearer Perspektiven und erweiterter Blickbeziehungen zum Himmel und zum Horizont – eine koordinierte Geometrie, die Räume und Materialien miteinander verbindet. Ein von einem Grundraster inspiriertes Gebäude, dessen Endlosigkeit sich in den langen Bürogängen, Raum- und Bewegungskorridoren, widerspiegelt. Zwischen den Platten wurden bewusst sichtbare Fugen gelassen, um Individualität und Linienstruktur deutlich zu machen. Dieser Bau setzt neue Standards für die Architektur des 21. Jahrhunderts in Dubai – lokal verankert, ohne aufgesetztes Thema und in einem Maßstab, der es eher wie ein urbanes Gebäude aus der Nachbarschaft und nicht wie einen anonymen Standardstadtturm wirken lässt.

[George Katodrytis]

GODWIN AUSTEN JOHNSON

National Federal Council –
New Parliament Building Complex / Abu Dhabi

designed by Ehrlich Architects in association
with Godwin Austen Johnson

~ GAJ is one of the largest and longest-established UK architectural and design practices in the UAE. Throughout its 20-year history, the company has created some of Dubai's most prominent buildings and helped define the Emirate as it is known today. The award-winning, multi-disciplinary architecture practice has particular expertise in the hotel and hospitality, residential and commercial, education, sport and leisure sectors – and its portfolio of work is extensive, with a wide range of built and ongoing projects across the Middle East and North Africa region.

~ GAJ ist eines der größten britischen Architekturbüros in den VAE. In seiner 20-jährigen Geschichte hat das Büro einige der prominentesten Gebäude errichtet und dazu beigetragen, das aktuelle Bild der Emirate zu definieren. Mit vielen Preisen ausgezeichnet und interdisziplinär tätig, plant das renommierte Büro Hotels und Restaurants, Wohn- und Gewerbebauten, Bildungs-, Sport- und Freizeiteinrichtungen – die Bandbreite der Arbeiten ist groß und die Zahl der realisierten und aktuellen Projekte im Nahen Osten und Nordafrika ist beeindruckend.

~ NATIONAL FEDERAL COUNCIL
NEW PARLIAMENT BUILDING COMPLEX
Ongoing

The UAE promotes an internationally recognised programme of social, economic and environmental sustainability. This new government complex will house the UAE's Federal National Council, a Parliamentary advisory body currently undergoing democratic constitutional reform. The project harmonises familiar Islamic design language with contemporary form and sustainable strategies, creating meaning and optimum function. Passive environmental methods employed for centuries by local builders are being integrated with cutting-edge technologies. The site of the building conveys its significance as a public institution. Facing the Arabian Gulf, the building's welcoming façade expresses the FNC's all-encompassing role in the life of Emirati citizens, as well as its increasing transparency, as the country moves towards democracy. The design is anchored by a 100-metre diameter dome – a contemporary descendant of the Hagia Sophia and Blue Mosque domes in Istanbul – representing the "flower of the desert", derived from the yellow-petalled desert bloom (the national flower of the UAE). Patterned with sunscreens and translucent stone panels, the structure cools and sheds dappled light of Islamic patterns on the Assembly Hall. A monolithic terraced plinth forms a massive square surrounding the circular dome and Assembly Hall – with thick limestone exterior walls containing deep-set window openings, a sensible solution to the searing desert temperatures.

Die VAE fördern ein international anerkanntes Programm für Nachhaltigkeit in Gesellschaft, Wirtschaft und Umwelt. In diesem neuen Regierungskomplex wird der Nationalrat der VAE tagen, ein parlamentarisches Beratungsgremium, das derzeit nach demokratischen Verfassungsregeln reformiert wird. Der ausdrucksstarke und höchst funktionale Bau verbindet eine vertraute islamische Gestaltungssprache mit zeitgenössischen Formen und Strategien zur Nachhaltigkeit. Passive ökologische Maßnahmen, die von örtlichen Baumeistern seit Jahrhunderten realisiert werden, finden ebenso Verwendung wie modernste Technologien. Der Standort des Gebäudes vermittelt dessen Bedeutung als öffentliche Einrichtung. In der auf den Persischen Golf ausgerichteten einladenden Fassade des Gebäudes drückt sich die alles umfassende Rolle der Nationalversammlung für die Bürger der Emirate sowie deren zunehmende Transparenz auf dem Weg des Landes zur Demokratie aus. Kern- element des Entwurfs ist eine Kuppel mit einem Durchmesser von 100 m, die in zeitgenössischer Weise an die Kuppeln der Hagia Sophia und der Blauen Moschee in Istanbul erinnert und die „Wüstenblume", abgeleitet von den gelben Blütenblättern der Nationalblume der VAE, darstellt. Die transluzenten, durchbrochenen Steinplatten dienen als Sonnenschutz und werfen in einem Spiel aus Licht und Schatten islamische Muster auf die Versammlungshalle. Ein monolithischer stufenförmig angelegter Sockel bildet einen kompakten Platz um die runde Kuppel und die Versammlungshalle. Als sinnvolle Antwort auf die glühende Hitze in der Wüste liegen die Fenster tief in den dicken Kalksteinwänden.

ZAHA HADID ARCHITECTS

Signature Towers / Dubai
Sheikh Zayed Bridge / Abu Dhabi
Opus Office Tower / Dubai

~ Zaha Hadid is internationally renowned for her built, theoretical and academic work. Each of her dynamic and innovative projects is built on over 30 years of revolutionary exploration and research in the fields of urbanism, architecture and design. Hadid's interest in the rigorous interface between architecture, landscape and geology steers the practice towards integrating natural topography and human-made systems – the result of a pioneering experimentation of cutting-edge technologies. Such a process has resulted in unexpected fluid, dynamic and complex architectural structures. The London-based studio continues to be a global leader in pioneering research and design exploration. Recently completed projects include the Nordpark Railway station in Innsbruck, the Mobile Art project for Chanel which travelled to Hong Kong, Tokyo and New York, the Zaragoza Bridge Pavilion in Spain and the Burnham Pavilion in Chicago.

~ Zaha Hadid genießt internationales Renommee, sowohl für ihre Bauten als auch für ihre theoretischen und wissenschaftlichen Arbeiten. Jedes ihrer dynamischen und innovativen Projekte greift auf über 30 Jahre Erfahrung mit revolutionären Forschungsarbeiten in den Bereichen Stadtplanung, Architektur und Design zurück. Hadids Interesse gilt der klaren Schnittstelle zwischen Architektur, Landschaft und Geologie und leitet sie, als Ergebnis wegweisender Experimente mit modernsten Technologien, zu der Einbindung der natürlichen Topografie und den von Menschen gemachten Systemen. Dieser Prozess führt zu unerwartet fließenden, dynamischen und komplexen Konstruktionen. Das Büro mit Hauptsitz in London ist immer noch weltweit führend im Bereich Forschung und neue Gestaltungsformen. Zu den in jüngster Zeit realisierten Projekten gehören der Bahnhof Nordpark in Innsbruck, das Mobile Art Project für Chanel, das in Hongkong, Tokio und New York gezeigt wurde, der Zaragoza Bridge Pavilion in Saragossa sowie der Burnham Pavilion in Chicago.

~ SIGNATURE TOWERS
Total Area: 350,000 m² above ground
Storeys: 75, 65, 51
Height: 357 m
Ongoing proposal

Zaha Hadid's design for the Signature Towers confirms the role of the Business Bay development at the forefront of Dubai's rapidly changing cityscape. The three towers rise above the creek and project themselves as an icon for the surrounding developments and the gulf region. The striking design creates a new presence that punctures the skyline with a powerfully recognisable silhouette. The fluid character of the towers is generated through an intrinsically dynamic composition of volumes. The towers are intertwined to share programmatic elements and rotate to maximise the views towards the creek and neighbouring developments. The design quality of the towers acts as a symbol which extends beyond their scale and location. These qualities derive from the boldness of the architectural concept, from the "choreographed" movement that combines the three towers in one overall gesture and "weaves" with a series of public spaces through the podium, the bridges and the landscape beyond. The programme was addressed as a whole with the three towers corresponding directly to the three main functions: office, residential and hotel. The towers share a common podium, designed as a materialised shadow of the towers and programmed with retail, restaurants and amenities that support the demands of the towers' population. The three towers are conjoined two by two, the offices and hotel at the base and the hotel and residences at the top. Through these adjacencies, the buildings are strategically organised in a symbiotic relation, sharing certain segments of the programme. Joining the three towers in one organism allows the development to be lived in a full day cycle.

Mit Zaha Hadids Entwurf für die Signature Towers erhält die sich rasch wandelnde Silhouette von Dubais Business Bay District einen weiteren Blickfang. Die drei am Fluss hoch aufragenden Türme werden mit ihrer eigenwilligen Form zu einem Wahrzeichen für die Umgebung und die Golf Region. Die markante Gestaltung erzeugt ein Gebäude mit starker Präsenz, das mit seiner weithin erkennbaren Form die Silhouette der Stadt prägen wird. Der fließende Charakter entsteht durch eine dynamische Komposition von Baukörpern. Die Türme sind gleichsam ineinander verschlungen, um gemeinsam Anforderungen aus dem Raumprogramm aufzunehmen und bestmögliche Aussichten auf den Fluss und die Umgebung zu bieten. Ihre großartige Gestaltung lässt sie zu einem Symbol werden, das über ihre eigene Größe und ihren Standort hinausweist. Das mutige Baukonzept und die dynamische Inszenierung verbinden die drei Türme zu einer einzigen großen Geste und betten sie ein in eine Reihe öffentlicher Räume wie den Sockelbau, die Brücken und die Landschaft dahinter. Das Raumprogramm findet in den drei Türmen, die den drei Hauptfunktionen – Büro, Wohnen und Hotel – zugeordnet sind, seine unmittelbare Entsprechung. Im gemeinsamen Sockelbau, der als Stein gewordener Schatten der Türme gestaltet ist, befinden sich Geschäfte, Restaurants und Freizeiteinrichtungen für die Bewohner. Jeweils zwei Türme sind miteinander verbunden, Büro- und Hotelturm im unteren Bereich und Hotel- und Wohnturm im oberen Bereich. Durch diese Verbindungen entsteht eine strategisch organisierte Symbiose, in der bestimmte Programmanforderungen geteilt werden. Die Verbindung der drei Türme zu einem Organismus bringt den Vorteil, dass die Anlage Tag und Nacht genutzt werden kann.

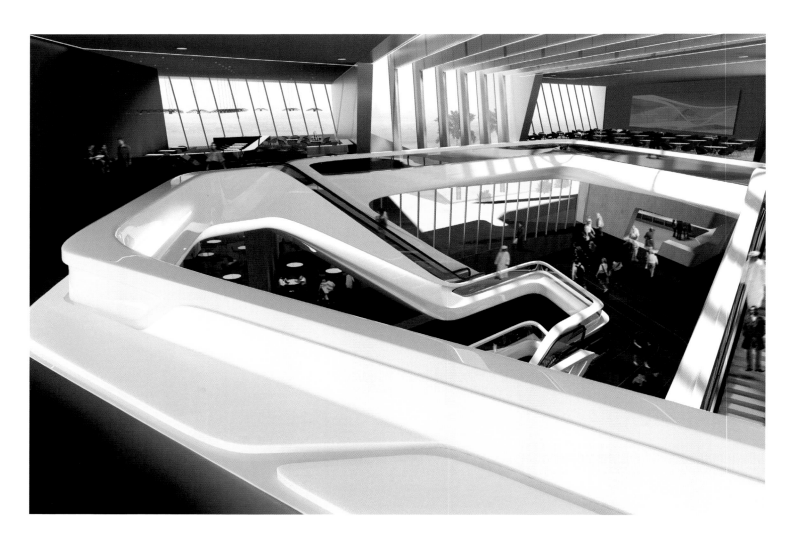

~ SHEIKH ZAYED BRIDGE
Dimensions: 842 m long, 64 m high, 61 m wide
Materials: piers, decking: reinforced concrete; arches: steel
Completion: 2011

The UAE has a highly mobile society that requires a new route around the Gulf's southern shore, connecting the Emirates together. In 1967 a steel arch bridge was built to connect the fledgling city of Abu Dhabi Island to the mainland, followed by a second bridge in the 1970s, connecting downstream to the south side of Abu Dhabi Island. The location of the third gateway crossing, close to the first bridge, is critical in the development and completion of the highway system. Conceived in an open setting, the bridge has the prospect of becoming a destination in itself and potential catalyst in the future urban growth of Abu Dhabi. A strand of structures gathered on one shore is lifted and propelled over the length of the channel. A biomorphic waveform provides the structural silhouette shape across the water. The mainland is the launch pad for the bridge structure emerging from the ground and approach road. The road decks are cantilevered on each side of the spine structure. Steel arches rise and spring from mass concrete piers asymmetrical in length between the road decks to mark the mainland and navigation channels. The spine splits and splays from one shore along the central void position, diverging under the road decks to the outside of the roadways at the other end of the bridge. The main bridge arch structure rises to a height of 60 m above water level with the road crowning to a height of 20 m above mean water level.

Die sehr mobile Gesellschaft der VAE benötigt eine neue Straße entlang der Südküste des Golfs, um die Emirate miteinander zu verbinden. 1967 wurde eine Stahlbogenbrücke zur Verbindung der neuen Stadt auf Abu Dhabi Island mit dem Festland gebaut, es folgte eine zweite in den 1970er-Jahren an der Südseite der Insel. Der Standort der dritten Brücke nahe der ersten ist wichtig für die Weiterentwicklung des Schnellstraßensystems. Als Solitär kann die Brücke durchaus selbst zu einem Besuchermagnet und zu einem Katalysator für das zukünftige Wachstum der Stadt werden. Wie Bänder, die an einem Ufer noch zusammengefasst sind und am anderen Ufer geteilt ankommen, bewegen sich die Bögen in einer biomorphen Welle, die der Brücke ihre markante Form verleiht, über den Kanal. Am Festland tauchen sie aus dem Boden auf und steigen zur Straße und über sie hinaus auf. Die Fahrbahnen hängen seitlich an diesen Bogenbändern; als Stahlbögen wachsen sie aus den massiven Betonstützen, asymmetrisch geformt, zwischen den Fahrbahnen heraus und verweisen damit auf das Festland und die Fahrrinne. Das Bogenband teilt sich, taucht zwischen den Fahrbahnen in den Uferboden ein und an der Außenseite der Fahrbahnen wieder auf. Der Hauptbogen der Brücke erreicht eine Höhe von 60 m über dem Wasser, die Straße verläuft 20 m über dem Wasser.

~ OPUS OFFICE TOWER
Total Built-up Area: 84,345 m²
Dimensions: 67 m long, 93 m high, 100 m wide
Storeys: 21
Materials: concrete
Bridge: steel structure
External façade: glass, sputter coated with a mirror pattern
Void façade: tinted grey glass
Ongoing

The realisation of the Business Bay masterplan is a monumental attempt to modify and evolve the existing urban fabric of Dubai. It proposes a series of striking buildings connected by low-rise podia and streets that together with the canal, create a unified whole. Two plots are interlinked by a continuous low-level podium structure which essentially unites the project and provides the unique possibility for interpreting the project as one mass. The two buildings take the form of a cube hovering off the ground, which is carved or eroded by a free-form void – essentially the setback space between the two tower envelopes. It is structured by a conventional system of slabs stacked vertically, serviced by central cores allowing for the areas near the façade to be occupied on all eight sides. The void, which is treated as a volume in its own right, being the space inside the build-mass, is free form and fluid and cuts through the edges of the cube, appearing as if it extends beyond the immediate boundaries of the cube. The interior of the void is clad in tinted double-glazing allowing for views into the void. The external plateaux within the void will be accessible to provide areas for recreation and relaxation. The interchange of perception of the tower at night is an important factor in the design: while the cube appears full with the void empty during the day, at night perception is one of opposites – where the cube appears dark and dematerialised, while the void could be activated with light, making it visible from afar.

Die Umsetzung des Masterplans für den Business Bay District ist ein Kraftakt zur Veränderung und Entwicklung bestehender urbaner Strukturen in Dubai. Vorgesehen sind darin eine Reihe herausragender Gebäude, die durch niedrige Sockelbauten und Straßen verbunden werden und zusammen mit dem Kanal ein einheitliches Ganzes schaffen. Zwei Grundstücke sind durch einen durchlaufenden, niedrigen Sockelbau miteinander verbunden, der das Projekt zu einer Einheit werden lässt. Die beiden Gebäude bilden zusammen einen Kubus, der über dem Boden zu schweben scheint und dessen unregelmäßig geformter, von beiden Türmen umhüllter offener Kern aussieht, als sei er herausgeschnitten worden oder durch Erosion entstanden. Die Türme besitzen eine konventionelle Konstruktion aus vertikal geschichteten Platten mit zentralen Versorgungskernen, so dass an allen acht Seiten nutzbare Flächen entlang der Fassade entstehen. Der offene Kern ist ein eigener Baukörper, ein Raum innerhalb der Baumasse, eine freie, fließende Form, die den Kubus über seine Ränder hinaus durchbricht. Die Abgrenzung von offenem Kern und hüllendem Gebäude bilden getönte Doppelscheiben, die einen Blick in das Kerninnere erlauben. Die Außenplateaus darin sind Erholungs- und Freizeitbereiche. Die Wahrnehmung des Turms verändert sich mit den Lichtverhältnissen: Während der Kubus tagsüber ausgefüllt und der Kern leer wirkt, ist es nachts umgekehrt – der Kubus erscheint dunkel und entmaterialisiert, und der Kern ist voller Licht und weithin sichtbar.

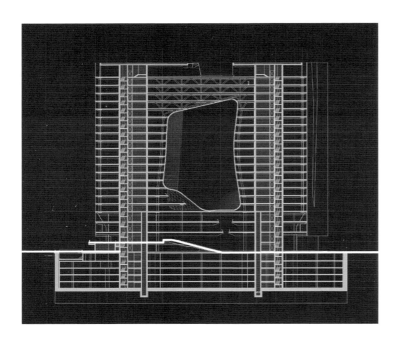

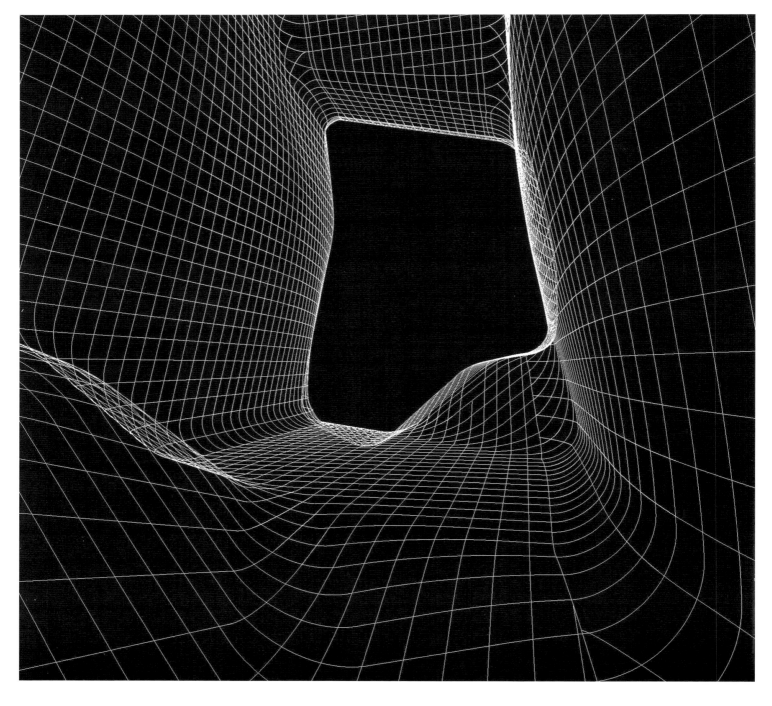

GLENN HOWELLS ARCHITECTS

55°TimeDubai / Dubai

with P&T Architects

~ Glenn Howells Architects has established a reputation over the last 20 years for delivering award-winning, high-quality projects. The UK practice has won a string of design competitions and, in addition to being shortlisted for the RIBA Stirling Prize (2007) and winning the British Council for Offices Best of the Best Award in 2010, has received over 60 national awards. With offices in Birmingham and London, the firm's expertise is drawn upon for masterplanning, infrastructure and feasibility studies, through to concept and full architectural construction design, as well as landscape and urban design.

~ Glenn Howells Architects hat sich in den vergangenen 20 Jahren mit vielen ausgezeichneten, qualitätvollen Projekten einen Namen gemacht. Das britische Büro hat eine Reihe von Wettbewerben gewonnen, war für den RIBA Stirling Prize 2007 nominiert, wurde 2010 vom British Council for Offices mit dem Best of the Best Award ausgezeichnet und erhielt 60 weitere nationale Preise. Die Niederlassungen in Birmingham und London beschäftigen sich insbesondere mit Städtebau, Infrastrukturuntersuchungen, Machbarkeitsstudien sowie Landschafts- und Stadtplanung; sie planen Gebäude von der ersten Konzeptidee bis zur Realisierung.

5.00 AM

1.00 PM

3.00 PM

4.00 PM

7.00 PM

8.00 PM

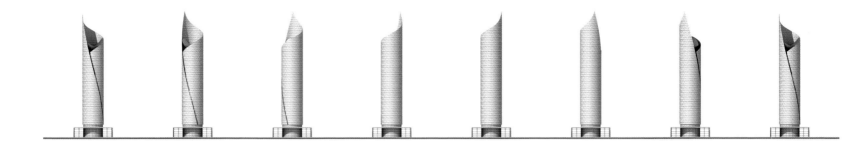

~ 55°TIMEDUBAI
Developer: 360°TimeWorld Ltd
Rotation Technology: Atkins Global (formerly M.G. Bennett & Associates)

Once completed, 55°TimeDubai will be the first of 24 prestigious residential buildings called Timepieces which are planned to be built in the world's major cities. Future Timepieces include: 115°TimeLasVegas, 74°TimeNewYork, 0°TimeLondon, 2°TimeParis, 73°TimeMumbai, 121°TimeShanghai. Named after their longitudinal lines, the towers slowly rotate around their vertical axes to offer panoramic 360-degree views – so providing visitors and residents with an unparalleled experience and views of the building's entire surroundings. The construction of 55°TimeDubai is taking place within a 7,300 m² master plot that will be surrounded by an expanse of tranquil landscape. The 30-storey tower will be positioned almost in the centre of a 20 m tall square base. The cylindrical structure will be wrapped in a ventilated double-skinned transparent wall that emphasises the tower's dynamism. The glass skin has diagonal gaps to help reduce air-conditioning loads. The environmentally sustainable tower smoothly glides in a clockwise direction. With solar energy powering its rotation, it moves approximately 52 degrees per day, at a speed of 63 cm per minute (two degrees per hour) – completing the cycle in a week as imperceptibly as a precision instrument. The building will revolve by means of 20 electric motors mounted on a system of ball bearings with an overall diameter of 29 m coated with a special polymer to reduce friction on the tracks during motion. The rotation machine is a modular construction, made up of equally sized identical planer machine track sections that are specifically designed to lock in and assemble on the perimeter of the tower's base. To ensure sustainability, the modular sections are designed to be removable, should parts need servicing, or a module element break down. This allows for the rotation machine to be replaced in sections, without affecting the tower's structure. Unlike other architectural structures, Glenn Howells Architects started from the inside out. The residential units will be located in sections of the ring-shaped outer area of the tower and, keeping the residents' experience in mind, expansive 14 m floor-to-ceiling windows help measure the passing of a day.

Das 55°TimeDubai wird nach seiner Fertigstellung das erste von 24 luxuriösen, Timepieces genannten Wohnhochhäusern sein, die in den großen Metropolen der Welt errichtet werden sollen. Zu den bisher geplanten Projekten gehören das 115°TimeLasVegas, 74°TimeNewYork, 0°TimeLondon, 2°TimeParis, 73°TimeMumbai und das 112°TimeShanghai. Nach ihrem Längengrad benannt, drehen die Türme sich langsam um ihre Senkrechte und gewähren Bewohnern wie Besuchern das einzigartige Erlebnis eines 360°-Panoramas. Das Gebäude in Dubai wird auf einem 7300 m² großen Grundstück errichtet, umgeben von einer harmonisch gestalteten Grünfläche. Der 30 Stockwerke zählende Turm steht, nahezu mittig positioniert, auf einem 20 m hohen, rechteckigen Grundsockel. Der zylindrische Baukörper ist von einer hinterlüfteten und transparenten doppelten Vorhangfassade eingefasst, die die dynamische Ausstrahlung des Gebäudes betont. Um den Aufwand für die Klimatisierung des Gebäudes zu verringern, ist die Glashaut von diagonalen Streifen durchbrochen. Mit einer Geschwindigkeit von 63 cm pro Minute dreht sich das Gebäude ungefähr um 52° pro Tag bzw. um 2° pro Stunde. Ähnlich den Bewegungen eines Präzisionsinstruments, die für den gelegentlichen Beobachter kaum merklich sind, vollzieht sich eine gesamte Umdrehung im Laufe einer Woche. Angetrieben wird der Rotationsmechanismus von 20 Elektromotoren, die auf einer Kugellagerkonstruktion von 29 m Durchmesser installiert sind. Zur Reduktion der Reibung sind die einzelnen Lager mit einem speziellen Polymer beschichtet. Der Strom kommt aus einer Solaranlage. Die in modularer Bauweise konstruierte Rotationsmaschine besteht aus gleich großen und identischen ebenen Gleisrahmen, die so konzipiert wurden, dass sie sich auf dem äußeren Rand des Turmsockels zusammenfügen lassen. Ferner können die Module, im Sinne der Nachhaltigkeit, für Reparaturen oder bei Materialversagen einzeln ausgebaut werden, ohne dass das Tragwerk des Turms beeinträchtigt würde. Im Gegensatz zur üblichen Konstruktionsweise gingen die Architekten des Büros Glenn Howell Architects bei ihrem Entwurf von innen nach außen vor. Die Wohneinheiten sind in den ringförmigen äußeren Elementen des Turms untergebracht. Riesige, 14 m hohe Fenster, die vom Boden bis zur Decke reichen, sorgen dafür, dass die Bewohner das Erlebnis einer sich ständig wandelnden Rundumsicht nahezu ungehindert genießen können.

LAVA

Snowflake Tower / Abu Dhabi

~ LAVA was founded in 2007 by Chris Bosse, Tobias Wallisser and Alexander Rieck, and operates as an architectural think-tank from Stuttgart and Sydney. At the vanguard of a new generation of architecture, the company's aim is to bridge the gap between the dream and the reality. LAVA believes that every architectural project contributes to the wider culture of architecture that carries a greater responsibility to its public and the environment. Using the latest advances in computing and building technology, LAVA wants to reposition the role of man in the natural environment.

~ LAVA wurde 2007 von Chris Bosse, Tobias Wallisser und Alexander Rieck gegründet und ist eine Denkfabrik im Bereich Architektur mit Sitz in Stuttgart und Sydney. Sie stehen an der Spitze einer neuen Generation von Architekten und möchten Traum und Realität miteinander verbinden. Nach der Überzeugung von LAVA ist jedes Bauprojekt Teil einer umfassenden Baukultur und der Architekt trägt dementsprechend eine große Verantwortung für das öffentliche Leben und die Umwelt. Durch den Einsatz modernster Computer- und Bautechnologie möchte LAVA die Rolle des Menschen in seiner natürlichen Umgebung neu definieren.

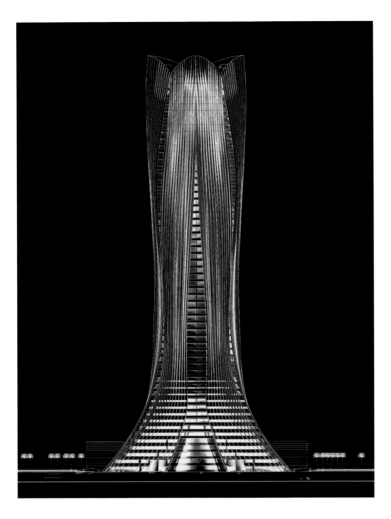

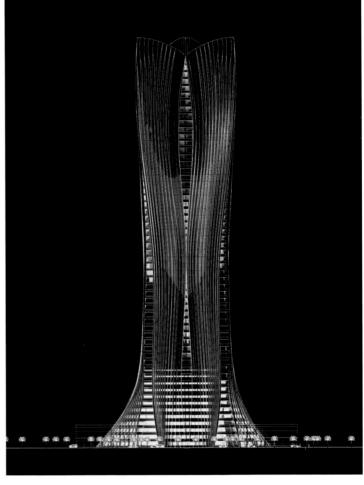

~ SNOWFLAKE TOWER
Client: PNYG Company
Height: 240 m
Ongoing

Developed as a prototype building translating brand values into an iconic architecture, this series of branded towers will be located at strategically chosen sites around the world. The synergies created by LAVA's distinctive thinking in architecture and marketing open up previously undiscovered dimensions in value creation for architectural developments. LAVA creates a complete environment, where design and brand become one. Despite the giant leaps in technology, outdated high-rise towers continue to dominate our cities. This branded tower will be their successor, redressing the ecological balance. With intelligent skins and systems, the structure can react to the external influences such as air-pressure, temperature, humidity, solar radiation and pollution. New materials and technology will be used to create robust, lightweight structures that adapt to and harmonise with their surroundings. The basic development principle will be adjusted to each specific location, generating a mix of local and global values. Collaborations with renowned furniture manufacturers will contribute to a well-executed and highly desirable environment, creating a new type of brand experience.

Weltweit soll an ausgewählten Standorten eine Serie von Hochhaustürmen entstehen, die als Marke erkennbar ist und dessen Prototyp die Werte dieser Marke als ikonenhafte Architektur vorgibt. Die Synergien, die durch einen für LAVA typischen Denkansatz hinsichtlich der Verbindung von Architektur und Marketing entstehen, eröffnen bislang noch unerkannte Dimensionen bei der Wertschöpfung im Bereich Architektur. LAVA schafft ein ganzheitliches Umfeld, in dem Design und Marke eins werden. Trotz gewaltiger technologischer Fortschritte bestimmen technisch veraltete Hochhäuser weiterhin die Städte. Dieser Markenturm wird ihre Nachfolge antreten und das ökologische Gleichgewicht wieder herstellen. Mit einer intelligenten Außenhaut und entsprechenden Versorgungssystemen kann die Konstruktion auf äußere Einflüsse wie Luftdruck, Temperatur, Feuchtigkeit, Sonneneinstrahlung und Luftverschmutzung reagieren. Neue Materialien und Technologien werden eingesetzt, um widerstandsfähige, leichte Konstruktionen zu erhalten, die sich an ihre Umgebung anpassen und sich harmonisch in diese einfügen. Das grundlegende Bauprinzip wird an jeden Standort speziell angepasst, um auf diese Weise lokale und globale Zielsetzungen zusammenzuführen. Die Zusammenarbeit mit renommierten Möbelherstellern trägt zu einem schönen und lebenswerten Umfeld bei, wodurch eine neue Form der Wahrnehmung einer Marke entsteht.

MASDAR CITY

Foster+Partners / Masdar Masterplan & Masdar Institute
LAVA / Masdar Plaza (Competition winning entry)

~ Masdar City, being constructed 17 km from downtown Abu Dhabi, is a brand-new enclave for renewable energy and clean technologies – where people can thrive, businesses can prosper, and innovation can flourish. A modern Arabian city that, like its forerunners, is in tune with its surroundings. A community where cutting-edge clean-tech research, pilot projects, building materials and technology testing and construction of some of the world's most sustainable buildings is now underway. Masdar City offers a fertile environment that inspires creativity and growth to organisations operating in this strategic and dynamic sector. Construction began in early 2008, thereby embodying Abu Dhabi's commitment to a sustainable future, while also pioneering the best practices in sustainable urban planning, design, development and operation. Two years on, Masdar City opened its first buildings, when the Masdar Institute of Science and Technology moved from its temporary facilities in Abu Dhabi to the new permanent campus in Masdar City. To be completed in stages, Phase 1 includes the Masdar headquarters, which will also house the International Renewable Energy Agency (IRENA); a second delivery of buildings for the Masdar Institute campus; the 10,000 m² Courtyard Building and other residential, commercial and retail developments and infrastructure. The remaining phases are expected to be completed by 2025. The phasing of construction is planned on a neighbourhood scale, so that finished sections will contain all necessary services and amenities, and won't be impacted by ongoing construction elsewhere. As a magnet for talent, financial capital and entrepreneurship in the fast-evolving renewable energy and clean-tech industry, Masdar City will provide a unique competitive advantage for companies, organisations and ancillary service providers operating in the city. As an industry cluster, the city is expected to be a dynamic, vibrant, international and entrepreneurial community that offers numerous benefits, including potential access to capital, a critical mass of sector knowledge, a large pool of high-quality talent, and a launch pad into local, regional and international markets. Significantly, Masdar City serves as an open technology platform that gives partner companies an unmatched opportunity to develop, test and validate their technologies in a large-scale, real-world environment – with particular consideration to the region's climate conditions and consumption patterns. Masdar City will immerse firms and employees in a community of like-minded professionals, as well as a physical surrounding that will be one of the world's most sustainable living and working environments. Power will come through a combination of sources, including photovoltaics, while thermal energy is being piloted for use in cooling. Energy consumption will be reduced through a range of passive and active technologies, including smart appliances, metres and grids, building management systems and building design and orientation. Sophisticated, state-of-the-art conservation, processing and reuse systems will reduce water consumption, and provide irrigation for landscaping. Waste will be processed, recycled and composted to a significant level. Transportation within Masdar City will primarily rely on electric buses, passenger cars and other clean-transport solutions, with the design of the city enabling individuals to live and work without the need for a personal vehicle. Masdar City is one of five integrated units of Masdar, a new kind of energy company based in Abu Dhabi that takes a holistic approach to the development, commercialisation and deployment of renewable and alternative energy technologies and solutions. Integrating research, development and innovation with investment, sustainable production, deployment and export, Masdar is a supporting pillar of the Abu Dhabi Economic Vision 2030, which seeks to diversify the local economy as it transitions from a natural resource-based economy to one that is largely knowledge-based. The company serves as a link between today's fossil fuel economy and the energy economy of the future – developing the "greenprint" for how we will live and work tomorrow.

[Alan Frost]

~ Masdar City, 17 km vom Stadtzentrum Abu Dhabis entfernt, ist eine brandneue Enklave für erneuerbare Energien und nachhaltige Technologien, ein Ort, wo Menschen sich entfalten, Unternehmen wachsen und Innovationen gedeihen können. Und eine moderne arabische Stadt, die wie ihre historischen Vorbilder den Einklang mit ihrer Umgebung sucht. In dieser neuen urbanen Gemeinde wird nicht nur modernste Forschung für saubere Technologien betrieben, hier ist auch Platz für Pilotprojekte zum Testen von neuen Materialien und Techniken: Gegenwärtig sind in Masdar City mehrere Gebäude im Bau, die in puncto Nachhaltigkeit Weltspitze sind. Bei den Unternehmen und Organisationen, die hier in diesem strategisch wichtigen und dynamischen Wirtschaftssektor tätig sind, wirkt die inspirierende Umgebung der Modellstadt kreativitäts- und wachstumsfördernd. Mit dem Baubeginn Anfang 2008 ließ Abu Dhabi seinem Bekenntnis zu einer nachhaltigen Zukunft Taten folgen. Die modernsten Methoden und neuesten Erkenntnisse in nachhaltiger Stadtplanung und Architektur kommen hier zum Einsatz – auf der Ebene der Entwicklung ebenso wie im täglichen Arbeitsbetrieb. Zwei Jahre später wurden in Masdar City die ersten Gebäude eröffnet, als das Masdar Institute of Science and Technology von seinem früheren Standort in Abu Dhabi auf den neuen Campus in Masdar City umzog. Die Fertigstellung ist in Stufen geplant: Phase 1 umfasst die Masdar-Zentrale, in der auch die Internationale Organisation für erneuerbare Energien (IRENA) untergebracht ist; zur zweiten Phase gehören Gebäude für den Campus des Masdar Institute sowie das 10.000 m² große Courtyard Building und eine Reihe von Wohn-, Büro- und Geschäftsgebäuden inklusive Infrastruktur. Die späteren Phasen werden bis 2025 abgeschlossen sein. Die Stufung des Bauprozesses orientiert sich an der Größe von Stadtvierteln. Fertiggestellte Stadtteile verfügen so über alle nötigen Anschlüsse und Versorgungseinrichtungen und werden nicht durch Bauarbeiten an anderer Stelle beein-

trächtigt. Als ein Ort, der auf Talente, Investoren und Unternehmer in der sich schnell entwickelnden Branche für erneuerbare Energien und saubere Technologien eine erhebliche Anziehungskraft ausübt, bietet Masdar City den niedergelassenen Technologiefirmen, Organisationen und Dienstleistern Wettbewerbsvorteile, die ihresgleichen suchen. Die Stadt ist ein dynamischer Industrie-Cluster, dessen lebendige internationale Unternehmergemeinschaft mit einer Vielzahl vor Vorteilen aufwartet: Zugang zu Kapital, eine Konzentration von branchenbezogenem Expertenwissen, ein großer Fundus an hochqualifizierten Fachleuten sowie hervorragende Verbindungen zu lokalen, regionalen und internationalen Märkten. Masdar City fungiert als offene Technologie-Plattform, die Partnerunternehmen einzigartige Gelegenheiten bietet, ihre neuen Technologien in einer realen Umgebung und in großem Maßstab zu entwickeln, zu testen und einzusetzen – mit besonderem Augenmerk auf die klimatischen Bedingungen der Region und auf Verbrauchsmuster. In Masdar City können Firmen und Mitarbeiter in eine Gemeinschaft von Fachleuten mit ähnlichen Interessen eintauchen; zugleich sind sie Teil einer der nachhaltigsten Wohn- und Arbeitsumgebungen weltweit. Strom wird auf verschiedene Arten produziert, u. a. in Photovoltaikanlagen. In einer Pilotanlage wird thermische Energie zur Kühlung verwendet. Für die Reduktion des Energieverbrauchs werden diverse passive und aktive Techniken genutzt: intelligente Geräte und Messuhren; Gebäudemanagementsysteme; Entwurf und Anordnung der Gebäude. Zur Senkung des Wasserverbrauchs kommen ausgeklügelte, hochmoderne Wasserspar- bzw. Aufbereitungs- und Rückführungssysteme zum Einsatz, die auch zur Bewässerung von Grünflächen herangezogen werden. Abfälle werden ebenfalls aufbereitet, recycelt und kompostiert. Der Transport innerhalb von Masdar City beruht hauptsächlich auf elektrischen Bussen und Pkws sowie anderen sauberen Verkehrsmitteln. Die Bewohner können ohne das eigene Auto zur Arbeit gelangen. Masdar City ist eine von fünf integrierten Einheiten von Masdar, einer Art Energiegesellschaft, die ihren Sitz in Abu Dhabi hat und bei der Entwicklung, Vermarktung und Implementierung von erneuerbaren Energien und sauberen Technologien einen ganzheitlichen Ansatz verfolgt. Mit ihrer Mission, Forschung, Entwicklung und Innovation mit Anlagestrategien, nachhaltiger Herstellung sowie Implementierungs- und Exportkonzepten zu verbinden, bildet Masdar eine der Säulen der „Abu Dhabi Economic Vision 2030". Ziel dieses Rahmenplans ist es, die lokale Wirtschaft durch Diversifizierung beim Übergang von einer auf Rohstoffexport gegründeten Struktur zu einer im Wesentlichen wissensbasierten Wirtschaft zu unterstützen. Masdar fungiert als Verbindungsglied zwischen der fossilen Brennstoffwirtschaft von heute und der Energiewirtschaft der Zukunft – eine Gesellschaft, die an der Vision einer „grünen" Lebens- und Arbeitswelt arbeitet.

[Alan Frost]

FACTS AT A GLANCE

Total Site Area: 5,900,000 m²
Total Gross Floor Area: 3,808,000 m²
Max. Building Height: 64 m
Average Floor Number: 4–6
Resident population: 40,000
Worker population: 50,000
Residential density: 150 persons/ha
City squares footprint: 280 ha
City squares (FAR): 1.8

STREET WIDTH

Central Spine: 25.0 m
Orbital Route: 15.6 m
Connector Streets: 12.0 m
Neighbourhood Streets: 10.5 m

LANDUSE PROGRAM

Residential: 52%
Commercial: 24%
Retail: 2%
Industrial: 12%
Community: 10%

~ FOSTER+PARTNERS / MASDAR MASTERPLAN

This mixed-use, low-rise, high-density development, strategically located for Abu Dhabi's transport infrastructure, will be linked to neighbouring communities and the international airport by existing road and rail routes. The surrounding land will contain photovoltaic farms and research fields, allowing the community to feed excess electricity back into the Abu Dhabi national grid. Inspired by the architecture and urban planning of traditional Arab cities, Masdar City incorporates narrow streets, the shading of windows, exterior walls and walkways, thick-walled buildings, courtyards and wind towers, vegetation and a generally walkable city. The design provides a high-quality living and working environment with a very low carbon footprint and includes a northeast–southwest orientation of the city. This makes the best use of the cooling night breezes and lessens the effect of hot daytime winds. There will be green parks separating built-up areas, not only to capture and direct cool breezes into the heart of the city but also to reduce solar gain and provide cool pleasant oases throughout the city. The intelligent design of residential and commercial spaces will reduce demand for artificial lighting and air conditioning. All buildings will meet high sustainable building standards. Carefully planned landscape and water features will aid in reducing ambient temperatures, while enhancing the quality of the street. An environment that prioritizes pedestrian travel not only makes the air cleaner but allows buildings to be closer together, providing more shade but allowing maximum natural light. The placement of residential, recreational, civic, leisure, retail, commercial and light industrial areas across the masterplan, along with the public transportation networks, will ensure that the city is pedestrian friendly and a pleasant and convenient place in which to live and work. The masterplan is designed to be highly flexible, to allow it to incorporate emergent technologies and to respond to lessons learnt during the implementation of the initial phases. Expansion has been anticipated from the outset, allowing for urban growth while avoiding the problem of sprawl that besets so many cities.

Diese Modellstadt zeichnet sich durch Mischnutzung, geringe Gebäude-
höhen und hohe Bebauungsdichte aus und ist verkehrstechnisch günstig
gelegen. Sie wird über bereits bestehende Straßen- und Schienenverbin-
dungen mit benachbarten Ortschaften und dem internationalen Flughafen
von Abu Dhabi verbunden. Die in der näheren Umgebung angesiedelten
Photovoltaikanlagen und Pilotanlagen für erneuerbare Energien werden
überschüssige Energie in das allgemeine Stromnetz von Abu Dhabi einspeisen. Von der Architektur und Stadtplanung alter arabischer Städte inspiriert, besticht Masdar City durch enge Straßen, sonnengeschützte Fenster, schattenspendende Außenmauern und Wege, dickwandige Gebäude mit kühlen Innenhöfen sowie durch Windtürme und Bepflanzung.
Generell ist die Stadt sehr fußgängerfreundlich. Ziel des Entwurfs war es,
ein Maximum an Qualität bei der Wohn- und Arbeitsumgebung mit einem
Minimum an CO_2-Ausstoß zu verbinden. Um die kühlende Brise der Nacht
zu nutzen und der Aufheizung durch die heißen Winde tagsüber entge-
genzuwirken, wurde die Stadt entlang einer Nordost-Südwest-Achse angelegt. Bebaute Zonen werden von begrünten Parkanlagen aufgelockert,
die nicht nur kühle Luft ins Stadtzentrum bringen, sondern auch der Erwär-
mung durch Sonneneinstrahlung entgegenwirken und angenehme, kühle
Oasen bilden. Dank einer intelligenten Planung bei Wohn- wie Geschäfts-

räumen verringert sich der Energieverbrauch durch künstliches Licht und
Klimatisierung. Sämtliche Gebäude sind auf die Erfüllung hoher Nach-
haltigkeitsstandards ausgelegt. Sorgfältig geplante Grünanlagen mit
Wasserelementen tragen ebenfalls zur Verringerung der Temperaturen
bei und erhöhen die Lebensqualität im urbanen Außenraum. Eine Stadt-
umgebung, die dem Fußgängerverkehr Vorrang gibt, verbessert nicht nur
die Luft, sondern ermöglicht auch ein engeres Zusammenrücken der Häu-
ser, was für mehr Schatten bei dennoch größtmöglichem natürlichen Lichteinfall sorgt. Die Anordnung und Verteilung von Wohngebieten, Erho-
lungs- und Freizeitzonen, Büros und Geschäften sowie Gebieten für leichte
Industrie auf dem im Masterplan ausgewiesenen Gelände und die Anbin-
dung dieser Zonen an ein öffentliches Verkehrsnetz wird die Stadt als einen
ausgesprochenen fußgängerfreundlichen Ort auszeichnen, an dem sich
angenehm leben und arbeiten lässt. Der Masterplan besteht aus einem
hochflexiblen Konzept, das es ermöglichen soll, noch im Entstehen begrif-
fene Technologien zu integrieren und Lerneffekte zu berücksichtigen, die
sich in den Anfangsphasen der Einführung ergeben. Erweiterungen der
Stadt sind von Anfang an vorgesehen. Dadurch kann Masdar City wachsen, gleichzeitig kann das Problem der Zersiedelung, mit dem so viele
Städte kämpfen, vermieden werden.

~ FOSTER+PARTNERS / MASDAR INSTITUTE
First phase completed: 2010 (started: 2007)

The Masdar Institute of Science and Technology is the first building in the Masdar City masterplan to be realised. It is an independent, research-driven graduate institute developed with the ongoing support and co-operation of the Massachusetts Institute of Technology (MIT). The Institute creates an educational focus for the entire programme, embodying the principles and goals of Masdar: to create a prototype sustainable city. The first building of its kind to be powered entirely by renewable solar energy during the day, the design incorporates a variety of passive and active environmental strategies and will be used as a test bed for the sustainable technologies that will be explored for implementation in future Masdar City buildings. The project signals Abu Dhabi's commitment to creating an international centre for pioneering sustainable technologies within an environment which is itself low-waste and low-carbon. The residences and laboratories are oriented to shade both adjacent buildings and the pedestrian streets below and the façades are self-shading. Over 5,000 m² of roof-mounted photovoltaic installations provide power and further protection from the sun. A 10 megawatt solar field within the masterplan provides energy for the Masdar Institute; any surplus is fed back to the Abu Dhabi grid. The campus will also use significantly less energy and water than average buildings in the UAE. Horizontal and vertical fins and brise soleil shade the laboratories, which have highly flexible "plug and play" services to encourage interdisciplinary research. These are highly insulated by façades of inflatable ETFE cushions, which remain cool to the touch under the intense desert sun. Cooling air currents are channelled through the public spaces using a contemporary interpretation of the region's traditional wind-towers, and green landscaping and water provide evaporative cooling. Windows in the residential buildings are protected by a contemporary re-interpretation of mashrabiya, a latticed projecting oriel window constructed with sustainably developed, glass-reinforced concrete and coloured with local sand to integrate with its desert context and to minimise maintenance. The perforations for light and shade are based on the patterns found in traditional Islamic architecture. The buildings' accommodations are supported by a variety of social or meeting spaces and landscaped areas that extend the civic realm. Low-rise, high-density apartment blocks act as a social counterpoint to the research environment.

Das Masdar Institute of Science and Technology ist das erste Gebäude, das im Rahmen des Masterplans für Masdar City realisiert wird. Es handelt sich um eine unabhängige Einrichtung, die sich hauptsächlich der Forschung widmet, mit Unterstützung des Massachusetts Institute of Technology (MIT) aufgebaut wurde und mit diesem dauerhaft kooperiert. Der Bau von Bildungseinrichtungen wird hier als zentraler Schwerpunkt des gesamten Projekts etabliert und verkörpert zudem dessen zugrunde liegendes Konzept von Masdar City, nämlich den Prototyp einer nachhaltigen Stadt zu errichten. Als erstes Gebäude seiner Art, das tagsüber ausschließlich mit erneuerbarer Solarenergie betrieben wird, wartet der Entwurf mit einer ganzen Reihe von aktiven und passiven Umwelteigenschaften auf und wird insofern als Prüfstand für die Nachhaltigkeitsstrategien fungieren, die auch in anderen geplanten Gebäuden der Musterstadt zum Einsatz kommen sollen. Mit der Errichtung eines internationalen Zentrums für nachhaltige Technologien an einem Ort, der selbst bereits als CO_2-arme und abfallvermeidende Umgebung konzipiert ist, unterstreicht Abu Dhabi sein Engagement für eine grüne Zukunft. Wohnungen und Labors sind so angeordnet, dass sie sowohl angrenzenden Gebäuden als auch den tiefer gelegenen Fußgängerzonen Schatten spenden; die Fassaden verschatten sich gegenseitig. Photovoltaikanlagen auf mehr als 5000 m² Dachfläche liefern Strom und zusätzlichen Sonnenschutz. Eine auf 10 Megawatt ausgelegte Solaranlage, die Teil des Masterplans ist, versorgt das Masdar Institute mit Elektri-

zität; überschüssige Energie wird in das Stromnetz von Abu Dhabi eingespeist. Auch der zugehörige Campus liegt mit seinem Wasser- und Energieverbrauch deutlich unter dem Durchschnitt anderer Gebäude in den VAE. Horizontale und vertikale Lamellen und Brise-Soleil-Systeme schützen die Labors, die mit ihren vielfältigen Plug-and-Play-Vorrichtungen zur interdisziplinären Forschung anregen, vor Sonneneinstrahlung. Die Fassaden sind mittels aufblasbarer EFTE-Kissen thermisch gut isoliert und fühlen sich, selbst wenn sie der intensiven Wüstensonne ausgesetzt sind, noch kühl an. In einer Art moderner Interpretation der traditionellen Windtürme der Region werden öffentliche Freiräume durch das Zuführen von Frischluft gekühlt. Grünflächen und Wasseranlagen sorgen mittels Verdunstung für weitere Abkühlung. In Wohngebäuden werden Fenster durch eine moderne Weiterentwicklung der Maschrabijja vor der Sonne geschützt: Diese Erkerfenster, gemäß Nachhaltigkeitskriterien entwickelt, sind aus mit Glas armiertem Beton gefertigt und mit lokalem Sand gefärbt. Sie fügen sich in die Wüstenlandschaft ein und erfordern kaum Instandhaltung. Die Perforationen, die das Spiel von Licht und Schatten bestimmen, greifen traditionelle Muster der islamischen Architektur auf. Neben den eigentlichen Wohnungen bieten die Gebäude diverse Räumlichkeiten für gemeinschaftliche Aktivitäten, auch die gestalteten Grünflächen außerhalb gehören dazu. Die niedrigen Gebäude mit hoher Wohndichte bilden einen sozialen Gegenpol zu den Arbeitsgebäuden der Forscher.

~ LAVA / MASDAR PLAZA
International design competition winning entry, 2009

As an "Oasis of the Future" this project proposes a living, breathing, active and adaptive environment, stimulated by the social interaction of people, and spotlighting the use and benefits of sustainable technology. Conceived as an open spatial experience, all features – hotel, conference, retail or leisure – offer the highest quality of comfort and interaction, with the Plaza being the social epicentre, offering 24-hour access to all facilities. Interactive, heat-sensitive technology activates low-intensity lighting in response to pedestrian traffic and mobile phone usage. The design seeks to accentuate user-experiences, marrying the lowest possible energy expenditure to the highest levels of user comfort in correlation to pedestrian flows. The ability to control ambient temperatures at all times of day is key to making the Plaza a compelling destination. The "Petals from Heaven" open and close to protect pedestrians from the sun, while capturing, storing and releasing the heat, adjusting the angle of shade depending on the position of the sun. Heat-sensitive lamps adjust the level of lighting to the proximity of pedestrians. Masdar Plaza will be a revolutionary venue within a visionary city.

Als „Oase der Zukunft" zielt dieser Entwurf auf ein lebendiges, atmendes, aktives und anpassungsfähiges Umfeld, das von der sozialen Interaktion der Menschen lebt und auf die Nutzung und den Nutzen nachhaltiger Technologien setzt. Die Oase ist ein überwältigender offener Raum, dessen sämtliche Elemente – Hotel, Konferenzräume, Geschäfte und Freizeiteinrichtungen – höchsten Komfort und beste Interaktionsmöglichkeiten bieten, wobei die Plaza das soziale Epizentrum mit Zugang zu allen Einrichtungen rund um die Uhr ist. Interaktive, wärmeempfindliche Technologien steuern die zurückhaltende Beleuchtung je nach Fußgängeraufkommen und Handynutzung. Die Gestaltung versucht, auf die Nutzer einzugehen und verbindet den geringstmöglichen Energieaufwand mit dem höchstmöglichen Nutzerkomfort in Korrelation zu den Fußgängerströmen. Die Möglichkeit der Steuerung der Umgebungstemperatur zu jeder Tageszeit ist von entscheidender Bedeutung für den Erfolg der Plaza. Die „Himmelsblüten", die sich nach der Sonne ausrichten, öffnen und schließen sich, um die Fußgänger vor der Sonne zu schützen; gleichzeitig nehmen sie auch Wärme auf, speichern sie und geben sie später wieder ab. Wärmeempfindliche Lampen passen die Beleuchtungsstärke der Nähe der Fußgänger an. Masdar Plaza wird ein revolutionärer Ort in einer visionären Stadt sein.

SAADIYAT CULTURAL DISTRICT, ABU DHABI

Ateliers Jean Nouvel / Louvre Abu Dhabi
Tadao Ando / Maritime Museum
Foster+Partners / Zayed National Museum
Gehry Partners / Guggenheim Abu Dhabi
Zaha Hadid Architects / Performing Arts Centre
Asymptote / Guggenheim Contemporary Art Pavilions
Studio Pei Zhu / Art Pavilion

District Land Area: 2,430,000 m²
Masterplan: Skidmore, Owings and Merrill
Development: TDIC

~ Saadiyat Island is a 27 km² area, 500 m northeast of Abu Dhabi, which is undergoing a remarkable transformation. In 2004, the Abu Dhabi Tourism Authority (ADTA) commissioned Tourism Development & Investment Company (TDIC) to create Saadiyat Island – a world-class tourist destination that included, as its centrepiece, a cultural district, within an environmentally sensitive framework. Just seven minutes from downtown Abu Dhabi and 20 minutes from Abu Dhabi International Airport, Saadiyat Island will be reached by two major bridges linking it with the mainland. Due for completion by 2018, the multi-faceted island is expected to be home to an estimated 150,000 residents with a full complement of leisure and tourism facilities, as well as civic and cultural amenities. Developed around seven districts – Saadiyat Cultural District, Saadiyat Beach, Saadiyat Retreat, Saadiyat Reserve, Saadiyat Marina, Saadiyat Promenade and Saadiyat Lagoons – the island will feature 29 hotels, 3 marinas, a cultural hub, 2 golf courses and 19 km of beachfront.

The Saadiyat Cultural District – an entire area on Saadiyat Island devoted to culture and the visual arts – is unprecedented in scale and scope, and with its exhibitions, permanent collections, productions and performances, will be an attraction of international calibre for local, regional and international visitors. The Cultural District will be home to five prestigious institutions as well as a park of pavilions, designed to host international art, architecture, and other cultural fairs and events. With an area of 270 hectares, the Cultural District will also boast city-facing quayside hotels, exclusive villas, and shops. The guiding principle for the Saadiyat Cultural District is to make it a must-visit destination for everyone involved in the world of art and culture. Working in collaboration with the US architectural firm Skidmore, Owings & Merrill, the TDIC developed Saadiyat Island's masterplan, and the Saadiyat Cultural District's set of permanent institutions is poised to offer the world's greatest concentration of cultural experiences.

The five key arts institutions are:

1. Performing Arts Centre designed by Zaha Hadid Architects: home of a multiplicity of genres and traditions of music, dance and theatre
2. Guggenheim Abu Dhabi designed by Frank Gehry Partners: a national platform for global contemporary art and culture that will present the most important artistic achievements of our time
3. Louvre Abu Dhabi designed by Ateliers Jean Nouvel: the first universal museum in the Arab world, designed to house the artistic expressions of different civilisations and cultures, from the most ancient to the most contemporary
4. Maritime Museum designed by Tadao Ando: a testament to the Arabian Gulf's maritime heritage
5. Zayed National Museum designed by Foster+Partners: the national museum of the UAE, telling the story of the late Sheikh Zayed bin Sultan Al Nahyan, his unification of the UAE, the history of the region and its cultural connections across the world.

~ Saadiyat Island ist ein 27 km² großes Gebiet 500 m nordöstlich von Abu Dhabi, auf dem sich große Veränderungen vollziehen. 2004 beauftragte die Tourismusbehörde von Abu Dhabi (ADTA) die Tourism Development & Investment Company (TDIC) mit der Planung von Saadiyat Island – einem ganz besonderen touristischen Ziel, in dessen Zentrum ein Kulturbereich, eingebettet in einen ökologischen Rahmen, stehen soll. Saadiyat Island ist nur sieben Minuten vom Zentrum Abu Dhabis und 20 Minuten vom Abu Dhabi International Airport entfernt und über zwei große Brücken mit dem Festland verbunden. Die Inselanlage soll 2018 fertiggestellt sein und 150.000 Menschen Wohnraum mit Freizeit-, Ausflugs- und Kultureinrichtungen und Versammlungsstätten bieten. Entstehen sollen sieben Distrikte: Saadiyat Cultural District, Saadiyat Beach, Saadiyat Retreat, Saadiyat Reserve, Saadiyat Marina, Saadiyat Promenade und Saadiyat Lagoons. Auf der Insel soll es 29 Hotels, drei Marinas, einen Kulturbereich, zwei Golfplätze und einen 19 km langen Strand geben.

Der Saadiyat Cultural District – ein eigener Bereich auf Saadiyat Island für Kultur und Kunst – ist von beispielloser Größe und wird mit seinen Ausstellungen, Sammlungen und Aufführungen internationale Bedeutung erlangen. Als Magnet für das lokale, regionale und internationale Publikum werden in dem Kulturdistrikt fünf angesehene Institutionen ihren Sitz haben; für den Pavillonpark sind internationale Kunst- und Architekturausstellungen und andere kulturelle Ereignisse geplant. Auf dem 270 ha großen Gelände wird es auch zur Stadt ausgerichtete Hotels am Kai, exklusive Villen und Geschäfte geben. Saadiyat Cultural District soll für alle Kunst- und Kulturbegeisterten das Reiseziel schlechthin werden. In Zusammenarbeit mit dem amerikanischen Architekturbüro Skidmore, Owings & Merrill erarbeitete TDIC den Masterplan für Saadiyat Island. Die dauerhaft im Saadiyat Cultural District residierenden Institutionen werden kulturelles Wissen in konzentrierter Form zur Verfügung stellen.

Die fünf großen Institutionen sind:

1. Performing Arts Centre von Zaha Hadid Architects: Musik, Tanz und Theater verschiedenster Genres und Traditionen
2. Guggenheim Abu Dhabi von Frank Gehry Partners: eine nationale Plattform für globale zeitgenössische Kunst und Kultur, auf der die wichtigsten aktuellen Kunstwerke präsentiert werden
3. Louvre Abu Dhabi von Ateliers Jean Nouvel: die erste Filiale in der arabischen Welt mit den künstlerischen Errungenschaften verschiedener Zivilisationen und Kulturen, von der Frühzeit bis heute
4. Maritime Museum von Tadao Ando: eine Hommage an das maritime Erbe der Golfstaaten
5. Zayed National Museum von Foster+Partners: das Nationalmuseum der VAE mit der Geschichte des verstorbenen Scheichs Zayed bin Sultan Al Nahyan und des Einigungsprozesses der VAE sowie der allgemeinen Geschichte der Region und ihrer weltweiten kulturellen Verbindungen.

~ ATELIERS JEAN NOUVEL / LOUVRE ABU DHABI
Usable Floor Area: 22,500 m²
Gross Floor Area: 63,000 m²
Estimated completion: 2014

The Louvre Abu Dhabi will be the first universal venue for the prestigious Paris-based museum, and will be the final destination of Saadiyat Island's cultural promenade. Born out of an agreement between the governments of the UAE and France, the Louvre Abu Dhabi will display art, objects and manuscripts of historical, cultural and sociological significance. The Louvre Abu Dhabi is also developing its own national collection which will be enriched by loans from French museums including Musée du Louvre, Musée d'Orsay and the Centre Pompidou. A shelter of light in the daytime, at night it takes the form of a sanctuary for the most valuable works of art. The spirit of the museum is materialised by ethereal white spaces punctuated with light. The building distinguishes itself by its sheer simplicity and sense of calm, and by a total rejection of plagiarised and overused historical and cultural themes. Ever aware of context, Nouvel designed a water system running through the museum, inspired by ancient Arabian engineering. The project is based on one of the key symbols of Arabic architecture – the Cupola – applying it in a modern design, far removed from anything traditional. With a 180-metre diameter, the doubled and flat dome offers a perfect luminous geometry, in a more random woven material to create a shadow punctuated with sun bursts. The Louvre Abu Dhabi Museum aims to be a welcoming world of light and shadow within a serene atmosphere. Its objective is to belong to its country, to its geography and to its history, avoiding the potentially dull translation of museum function which can result in predictability and convention. It also aims to emphasise the fascination generated by rare encounters. It is pretty unusual to find a built archipelago in the sea; it is even more unusual to find it protected by a parasol flooded with a rain of lights.

Der Louvre Abu Dhabi wird die erste Filiale des angesehenen, in Paris beheimateten Museums und der Endpunkt der Kulturpromenade auf Saadiyat Island sein. Seine Errichtung ist das Ergebnis einer Vereinbarung zwischen den Regierungen von den VAE und Frankreich. Das Museum wird Werke der bildenden Kunst und Manuskripte von historischer, soziokultureller Bedeutung ausstellen. Das Louvre Abu Dhabi baut darüber hinaus auch eine eigene nationale Sammlung auf, die durch Leihgaben aus französischen Museen, wie dem Musée du Louvre, dem Musée d'Orsay und dem Centre Pompidou, ergänzt wird. Während das Gebäude bei Tag die Exponate vor Licht schützt, ist es bei Nacht ein Sanktuarium für die äußerst wertvollen Kunstwerke. Der Geist des Museums manifestiert sich in ätherischen weißen Räumen, in die durch die perforierte Decke einzelne Lichtstahlen fallen. Das Besondere dieses Gebäudes ist seine Einfachheit und Ruhe sowie die konsequente Ablehnung abgedroschener historischer und kultureller Themen. Nouvel holt den Kontext in das Museum, in dem ein von der alten arabischen Ingenieurskunst inspiriertes Kanalsystem verläuft. Der Entwurf leitet sich aus einem der wichtigsten Elemente der arabischen Architektur – der Kuppel – ab, die Nouvel fernab von aller Tradition zeitgenössisch interpretiert. Die große flache Kuppel mit einem Durchmesser von 180 m wird mit ihren verschiedenen Lochmustern zu einer transluzenten Decke, durch die punktförmig Sonnenstrahlen in den schattigen Raum dringen. Das Louvre Abu Dhabi soll eine einladende Welt aus Licht und Schatten mit einer heiter-gelassenen Atmosphäre sein. Ziel ist es, Teil des Landes, seiner Geografie und Geschichte, zu werden. Um nicht im Vorhersehbaren und Konventionellen zu erstarren, soll darauf verzichtet werden, die klassischen Präsentations- und Vermittlungsaufgaben eines Museums auf den Louvre Abu Dhabi zu übertragen. Vielmehr soll dem Faszinosum ungewöhnlicher Begegnungen ein Raum eröffnet werden – so ungwöhnlich wie ein überbauter Archipel im Meer, überspannt von einem Sonnenschirm, durch den das Licht „tropft".

~ TADAO ANDO / MARITIME MUSEUM
Estimated completion: 2018

With obvious links to the sea, the Maritime Museum is located in the Cultural District's Marina. The museum will house the UAE's seafaring history, as well as providing a meeting point of land and sea, and the traditions of yesterday and tomorrow. The museum will celebrate Abu Dhabi's maritime heritage, exploring the country's long relationship with the sea. The deceptively simple building will combine space, light and water inside and out – seamlessly blending the building's interior and exterior to ensure that the Arabian Gulf is, fittingly, the museum's most stunning exhibit. The observation of Abu Dhabi's nature, landscape and maritime traditions served as the inspiration for the museum's design. Its elegant architecture is defined by a unique space in the form of a sail, full of wind, carved out of a simple volume. The solitary structure stands like a gate on a vast water court, defining a spacial encounter between two important landscape elements of the city: the land and the water. With its reflective surface, the water court visually merges site and sea, reinforcing the maritime theme of the museum. Within the ship-like interior, the ramps and floating decks will guide visitors through to the exhibition space. A traditional dhow will float over the voids of the museum's interior, featuring a magnificent underwater aquarium.

Schon durch seinen Standort in der Marina des Cultural District wird die Funktion des Maritime Museum augenfällig. An diesem Ort wird die Seefahrergeschichte der VAE präsentiert; hier treffen sich Land und Meer, Tradition und Zukunft – eine Hommage an das maritime Erbe von Abu Dhabi und die lange Beziehung des Landes zum Meer. Das innen und außen überraschend schlichte Gebäude kombiniert Raum, Licht und Wasser, wobei Innen- und Außenräume nahtlos ineinander übergehen und der Persische Golf selbst zum beeindruckendsten Exponat wird. Die Beobachtung der Natur, die Landschaft und die Seefahrertraditionen inspirierten die Gestaltung. Die elegante Architektur wird bestimmt von einem einzigartigen Raum in Form eines vom Wind geblähten Segels, wie herausgeschnitzt aus einem schlichten Baukörper. Der Solitär steht wie ein Tor in einem riesigen Hof aus Wasser und verkörpert die Begegnung von zwei wichtigen Landschaftselementen der Stadt: Land und Wasser. Mit seiner spiegelnden Oberfläche lässt der Wasserhof das Areal und das Meer miteinander verschmelzen und verstärkt das maritime Thema des Museums. Das Innere des Museum wirkt wie ein Schiff und Rampen und Stege führen die Besucher durch die Ausstellung. Eine traditionelle Dhau wird in den Museumsräumen schweben, in denen auch ein Unterwasseraquarium zu bewundern sein wird.

~ FOSTER+PARTNERS / ZAYED NATIONAL MUSEUM
Wings Height: 73–124 m
Gross Internal Area: 58,698 m²
Total Built-up Area: 66,042 m²
Total Gallery Space: 5,764 m²
Museum & Mound Site Area: 53,331 m²
Public Gardens, Total Area: 21,439 m²
Estimated completion: 2014

Conceived as a monument and memorial to the late Sheikh Zayed bin Sultan Al Nahyan, the founding president of the UAE, the Zayed National Museum will be the centrepiece of the Saadiyat Cultural District and will showcase the history, culture and, more recently, the social and economic transformation of the Emirates. Fittingly elevated above the rest of the Cultural District at its highest point, the museum will feature five galleries, each themed around a pillar of Sheikh Zayed's legacy and central aspects of his life's work. The museum will also encompass a presidential library, falconry centre, and a family theatre. The towers are lightweight steel structures, sculpted aerodynamically to work like the feathers of a bird's wing. Inside this structure, the gallery spaces are constructed as pods, which will be suspended above visitors passing through the ground floor lobby. The lobby will be part of an elevated mound that also incorporates a gallery dedicated to the life of Sheikh Zayed, a pavilion for special exhibitions and a falconry centre with live displays. The building is designed to minimise energy usage by incorporating natural ventilation and lighting in the five towers, and using photovoltaic panels and heat exchange technologies. Architecturally, the aim has been to combine a highly efficient, contemporary form with elements of traditional Arabic design and hospitality to create a museum that is sustainable, welcoming and culturally of its place. The solar thermal towers heat up and act as thermal chimneys to draw cooling air currents naturally through the museum. Fresh air is captured at low level and drawn through buried ground-cooling pipes and then released into the museum's lobby. The heat at the top of the towers works to draw the air up vertically through the galleries due to the thermal stack effect. Air vents open at the top of the wing-shaped towers taking advantage of the negative pressure on the lee of the wing profile to draw the hot air out. Balancing the lightweight steel structures with a more monumental interior experience, the galleries are anchored by a dramatic top-lit central lobby, which is dug into the earth to exploit its thermal properties and brings together shops, cafés, an auditorium and informal venues for performances of poetry and dance. Throughout, the treatment of light and shade draws on a tradition of discreet, carefully positioned openings, which capture and direct the region's intense sunlight to illuminate and animate these interior spaces. Objects are displayed within niches and on stone plinths that rise seamlessly from the floor.

Das Zayed National Museum ist als großes Denkmal für den verstorbenen Scheich Zayed bin Sultan Al Nahyan, dem Gründer und ersten Präsidenten der VAE, geplant und wird zentrales Bauwerk des Saadiyat Cultural District sein. Gezeigt werden darin die Geschichte, die Kultur und die jüngsten gesellschaftlichen und wirtschaftlichen Veränderungen der Emirate. Seiner Bedeutung entsprechend erhebt sich das Museum über den Cultural District und steht auf dem höchsten Punkt der Insel. Das Museum besteht aus fünf Abteilungen, denen jeweils ein Thema aus der Lebensphilosophie und zentrale Aspekte des Lebenswerks von Scheich Zayed zugeordnet sind. In dem Museum wird es auch eine Präsidentenbibliothek, eine Falknerei und ein Familientheater geben. Die Türme aus einer leichten Stahlkonstruktion sind aerodynamisch geformt und erinnern an Vogelfedern. Innen hängen die Ausstellungsräume wie Kapseln über den Besuchern, die durch die Lobby der Erdgeschossebene laufen. Leicht erhöht befinden sich die Eingangshalle, in der das Leben von Scheich Zayed gezeigt wird, ein Pavillon für Sonderausstellungen und die Falknerei mit echten Falken. Damit das Gebäude möglichst wenig Energie verbraucht, ist in den fünf Türmen eine natürliche Belüftung und Belichtung sowie der Einsatz von Solarmodulen und Wärmetauschern vorgesehen. Hocheffiziente moderne Formen werden verbunden mit Elementen der traditionellen arabischen Ästhetik und sollen so ein besucherfreundliches, vom Prinzip der Nachhaltigkeit geprägtes Museum schaffen. Die Thermo-Solar-Türme heizen sich auf und nutzen den Kamineffekt, um auf natürliche Weise kühlende Luftströme durch das Museum zu leiten. Frische Luft wird unten angesaugt, durch im Boden verlegte Kühlrohre geführt und dann in die Lobby geleitet. Durch die Wärme im oberen Bereich der Türme steigt die Luft senkrecht durch die Ausstellungsräume nach oben. Lüftungsklappen am oberen Ende der wie Flügel geformten Türme öffnen sich aufgrund des Unterdrucks auf der Leeseite des Flügelprofils, und die warme Luft kann entweichen. Um als Ausgleich zu der leichten Stahlkonstruktion einen monumentaleren Innenraum zu erhalten, hängen die Ausstellungsräume in einer spannungsvoll von oben belichteten zentralen Lobby, die aus thermischen Gründen in den Boden eingelassen ist und in der Geschäfte, Cafés, ein Auditorium und eine schlichte Bühne für Dichterlesungen und Tanzvorführungen zusammengefasst sind. In dem gesamten Komplex folgt die Behandlung von Licht und Schatten einer Tradition dezenter, wohlüberlegt platzierter Öffnungen, durch die das intensive Sonnenlicht dieser Region die Innenräume geschickt belichtet und lebendig werden lässt. Die Exponate stehen in Nischen und auf Steinsockeln, die aus dem Boden herauszuwachsen scheinen.

~ GEHRY PARTNERS / GUGGENHEIM ABU DHABI
Total Floor Area: 30,000 m²
Estimated completion: 2014

The Guggenheim Abu Dhabi will be the largest Guggenheim museum in the world. It will house its own major contemporary art collection and present special exhibitions featuring works from the Guggenheim Foundation's extensive collection. The museum will showcase international exhibitions and education programmes with a particular emphasis on Middle Eastern contemporary culture. Visitors will enter the museum through one of the building's cones, whose exterior is covered with blue glass panes and defined inside with a dynamic timber composition. Open to the elements, the Guggenheim's ABU DHABI cones recall the region's ancient wind-towers which both ventilate and shade the museum's exterior courtyards in a fitting blend of Arabic tradition and modernity, combined with sustainable design. The building defines a new approach to the museum visitor experience and presents an innovative vision for viewing contemporary art in the context of a desert landscape. The building site also serves as a man-made breakwater configured to protect the island's pristine north beach zone. The museum concept comprises a permanent collection and special exhibitions galleries, a centre for art and technology, and for contemporary Arab, Islamic and Middle Eastern culture, an education facility, a research centre, and a state-of-the-art conservation laboratory. Inspired by expansive industrial studio spaces, the museum design reflects the large scale at which many contemporary artists work, and presents new gallery layouts unlike conventional museum spaces. Surrounding a covered courtyard, clusters of galleries in varying heights, shapes and character allow for curatorial flexibility in organising exhibitions at dimensions that have not previously existed, creating an exciting range of exhibition spaces.

Das Guggenheim Abu Dhabi wird das weltweit größte Guggenheim Museum werden. Es wird seine eigene bedeutende Sammlung zeitgenössischer Kunst sowie Sonderausstellungen mit Arbeiten der umfangreichen Sammlung der Guggenheim Foundation zeigen. Außerdem werden internationale Ausstellungen zu sehen sein, und mit eigenen Programmen wird auf die Besonderheiten der zeitgenössischen Kultur des Nahen Ostens eingegangen werden. Der Hauptzugang zu dem Museum liegt in einem der Gebäudekegel, die außen mit blauen Glasplatten verkleidet sind und sich innen als dynamische Holzkomposition fortsetzen. Die offenen Kegel, die die Innenhöfe des Museums mit Frischluft versorgen und ihnen Schatten spenden, erinnern an die alten Windtürme dieser Region; sie lassen die arabische Tradition mit der Moderne sowie einer nachhaltigen Gestaltung verschmelzen. Das Gebäude steht für einen neuen Ansatz, die Aufmerksamkeit der Besucher zu fesseln und präsentiert eine innovative Vision, zeitgenössische Kunst im Kontext einer Wüsten-

landschaft zu betrachten. Das Gebäudeareal fungiert zudem als eine Art Wellenbrecher, mit dem die unberührte Küstenzone im Norden der Insel geschützt werden soll. Das Museum bietet Raum für eine Dauerausstellung und für Sonderausstellungen, ein Zentrum für Kunst und Technologie sowie für die zeitgenössische arabische und islamische Kultur sowie die Kultur des Nahen Ostens, ein Bildungszentrum, ein Forschungszentrum und ein hochmodernes Labor für Konservierungsarbeiten. Die Gestaltung des Museums ist inspiriert von ausgedehnten industriellen Atelierräumen und reflektiert damit die großen Maßstäbe, in denen viele zeitgenössische Künstler arbeiten. Um einen überdachten Innenhof gruppieren sich die Ausstellungsräume mit unterschiedlicher Raumhöhe, Form und Charakter. Die sich derart von konventionellen Museumsräumen absetzenden Ausstellungsräume ermöglichen den Kuratoren eine große Flexibilität bei der Organisation von Ausstellungen, die es so noch nie zuvor gegeben hat.

~ ZAHA HADID ARCHITECTS / PERFORMING ARTS CENTRE
Height: 62 m
Width: 135 m
Length incl. Bridge: 490 m
Total Floor Area: 62,770 m²
Footprint: 25,800 m² (excl. Bridge)
Five theatres
Seating capacity: 6,300
Levels: 10 above, 4 underground
Estimated completion: 2018

This multifunctional space will house five theatres: a music hall, concert hall, concert hall, opera house, drama theatre, an experimental performance space and an Academy of Performing Arts. Zaha Hadid's design for the Performing Arts Centre reflects the fluidity of motion, and is inspired by forms encountered in the natural world. The building has been designed to flow from the centre of the Saadiyat Cultural District, drawing visitors inside and conveying them upwards towards the performance spaces at the summit facing the Arabian Gulf. The Centre's distinct formal language is derived from a set of typologies evident in organisational systems and growth in the natural world. These natural scenarios are formed by energy being supplied to enclosed systems, and the subsequent decrease in energy caused when organised structures develop in nature. The "energy" of the Performing Arts Centre is symbolised by the predominant movements in the urban fabric along the central axis of the pedestrian corridor and the cultural centre's seafront promenade – the site's two intersecting primary elements. Growth simulation processes have been used to develop spatial representations into a set of basic geometries and then superimposed with programmatic diagrams into a series of repeated cycles. The primary components of this biological analogy (branches, stems, fruits and leaves) are then transformed from abstract diagrams into architectonic design. The central axis of Abu Dhabi's Cultural District is a pedestrian corridor that stretches from the Sheikh Zayed National Museum towards the sea. This axis interacts with the seafront promenade to generate a branching geometry where islands are formed, isolated and translated into distinct bodies within the Performing Arts Centre to house the main concert hall above the lower four theatres, allowing daylight into its interior and dramatic views of the sea and city skyline from the huge window behind the stage. Individual lobbies for each theatre are orientated towards the sea, giving visitors constant visual contact with their surroundings. The Academy for Performing Arts is housed above the Experimental Theatre in the southern side of the building whilst the eastern "tail" has retail areas taking advantage of pedestrian flow from the bridge that connects the Centre with the main artery of the Cultural District.

Im Performing Arts Centre werden fünf Bühnen untergebracht sein: ein Varieté, ein Konzertsaal, ein Opernhaus, eine Schauspielbühne und eine Bühne für experimentelle Veranstaltungen. Auch eine Akademie für darstellende Künste soll hier ihren Platz haben. Inspiriert von den Formen der Natur, spiegelt Zaha Hadids Entwurf eine fließende Bewegung wider, gleichsam jene Bewegung, mit der die Besucher aus dem Zentrum des Saadiyat Cultural District angezogen werden, um sie sodann hinauf zu den Bühnen hoch über dem Persischen Golf zu führen. Die besondere Formensprache ist abgeleitet von verschiedenen Typologien, wie sie in vielen Organisationssystemen und Wuchsformen der Natur vorkommen. Diese Bezüge zur Natur entstehen, wenn geschlossene Systeme mit Energie versorgt werden und dann die Energiezufuhr geringer wird, weil sich eine geregelte Struktur in der Natur entwickelt. Die „Energie" des Performing Arts Centre wird von den vorherrschenden Bewegungen im urbanen Gefüge entlang der zentralen Achse der Fußgängerstraße und der Uferpromenade des Kulturzentrums – die beiden sich kreuzenden Hauptelemente des Areals – symbolisiert. Wachstumssimulationsprozesse wurden eingesetzt, um aus geometrischen Grundformen, über die die Inhalte des Raumprogramms in einer Serie sich wiederholender Kreise gelegt wurden, Raumdarstellungen zu entwickeln. Die Hauptelemente dieser Bio-Analogie (Zweige, Stängel, Früchte und Blätter) werden dann aus abstrakten Diagrammen in gestaltete Architektur umgesetzt. Die zentrale Achse von Abu Dhabis Kulturdistrikt ist eine Fußgängerstraße, die sich vom Sheikh Zayed National Museum bis zum Meer erstreckt. Diese Achse interagiert mit der Uferpromenade und schafft so geometrische Abzweigungen, durch die Inseln geformt, abgetrennt und zu eigenen Körpern innerhalb des Performing Arts Centre werden; in diesen befindet sich der Hauptkonzertsaal über den darunter liegenden vier Theatern. Durch die riesigen Fenster hinter der Bühne kann Tageslicht in den Saal gelangen und bietet sich ein großartiger Blick auf das Meer und die Skyline der Stadt. Die Vorhallen für jedes Theater liegen auf der Meerseite, damit die Besucher optisch immer mit der Umgebung verbunden sind. Die Academy for Performing Arts befindet sich über dem Experimental Theatre auf der Südseite des Gebäudes; im „Gebäudeschwanz" im Osten sind Geschäfte untergebracht, die sich zu den Fußgängern auf der Brücke, die das Zentrum mit dem Hauptweg des Kulturdistrikts verbindet, öffnen.

~ ASYMPTOTE ARCHITECTURE /
GUGGENHEIM CONTEMPORARY ART PAVILIONS

A series of pavilions looks to the past, present and future, engaged in a profound and silent dialogue. Designed to embody a timelessness, they allow for varied subjective interpretations and meanings as time and local culture moves forward. Through their abstract and formal language, the pavilions are conceived as tectonic gestures, privileging elegance, perfection and beauty, drawn from the landscape, histories and futures that define this remarkable part of the world. The Guggenheim Pavilions were conceived of as cutting-edge "big box" contemporary art galleries. The architecture merges the region's rich cultural traditions with new spatial, technological and structural concepts – allowing for truly pioneering buildings. The two articulated "shell" enclosures primarily house viewing galleries for contemporary art in its many guises from traditional painting and sculpture to video and interactive installations, as well as virtual reality and electronic art forms. The galleries are designed as flexible and dynamic interior environments, utilising electronic enclosure designs that filter, modulate and refract external daylight and interior artificial illumination. The design of each pavilion is drawn from influences in nature as well as from the man-made environment. The stone and jewel-like qualities of the forms engender a timeless essence. Poised within the landscape, the inclined geometry of the forms invites visitors to slip beneath the polished surfaces towards the public entrances. Upon entering, the optical effects created through apertures in the enclosure capture the visitor's eye. Light within the pavilions is filtered and modulated to create vivid and vibrant environments for the exhibitions, while enhancing the spatial qualities created by the robust shell tectonics that encase the galleries, cafés and other public spaces.

Eine Reihe von Pavillons, die in einem intensiven und stillen Dialog miteinander stehen, erlaubt einen Blick in die Vergangenheit, Gegenwart und Zukunft. Ihre Gestaltung soll Zeitlosigkeit vermitteln, und indem die Zeit und die kulturelle Entwicklung vor Ort voranschreiten, lassen sie vielfältige eigene Interpretationen und Bedeutungen zu. Durch ihre abstrakte und formale Sprache fungieren die Pavillons auch als tektonische Gesten, die Eleganz, Perfektion und Schönheit feiern – inspiriert von der Landschaft, der Geschichte und der Zukunft, die diesen bemerkenswerten Teil der Welt formen. Die Guggenheim Pavillons sind zeitgenössische Kunstgalerien, gestaltet als hochmoderne „big box". In der Architektur verschmelzen die vielfältigen traditionellen Kulturen der Region mit neuen räumlichen, technologischen und konstruktiven Konzepten, woraus sich wahrhaft wegweisende Gebäude ergeben. Umhüllt von klar strukturierten „Schalen" sind in den beiden Gebäuden vor allem Ausstellungsräume für zeitgenössische Kunst in ihren vielen Ausprägungen untergebracht – von traditioneller Malerei und Bildhauerei bis hin zu Videoinstallationen und interaktiven Exponaten sowie Virtual Reality und Electronic Art. Die Innenräume der Galerien sind flexibel und dynamisch, sie nutzen elektronische Steuerelemente, um das Tageslicht und die künstliche Beleuchtung zu filtern, zu modulieren und zu brechen. Die Gestaltung jedes Pavillons ist sowohl von der Natur als auch von der vom Menschen gemachten Umwelt inspiriert. Die Formen, die an Natursteine und Edelsteine erinnern, schaffen eine tiefgründige Zeitlosigkeit. Die Pavillons liegen in der Landschaft, und ihre Schrägen laden die Besucher ein, unter den glänzend polierten Oberflächen durch die Eingänge zu schlüpfen. Die überwältigenden optischen Eindrücke ziehen den Eintretenden sofort in ihren Bann. Das gefilterte und modulierte Licht lässt lebendige, dynamische Ausstellungsräume entstehen und steigert die Raumqualität der robusten Schalenkonstruktion, in der die Galerien, Cafés und weitere öffentliche Räume untergebracht sind.

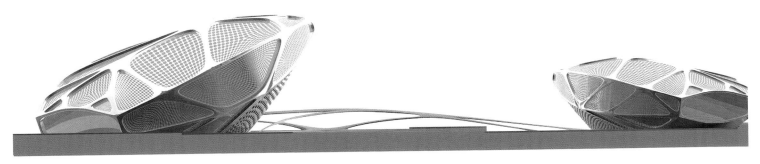

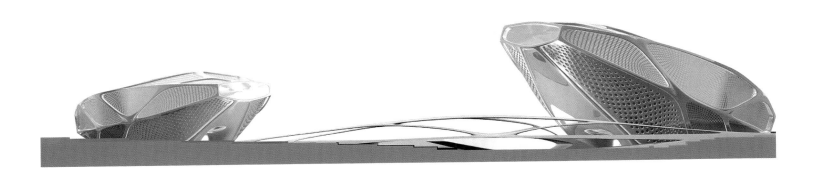

~ STUDIO PEI ZHU / ART PAVILION
Total Building Area: 3,500 m²

The design of this art pavilion aims to maximise the potential of its site by creating a dynamic connection between the urban fabric of the new Cultural District and the canal at the centre of the Biennale Park. Raising the main exhibition space above the park, a continuous public realm is created at ground level. This space is more than just a gateway to the exhibition space, or an alternative route between the street and canal; it is a place for curious passers-by to investigate while also being a location for small public events or performances. The walls rise up to enclose the exhibition space above a steeply outward slope, creating an external shaded area for park and pavilion visitors alike to enjoy, and maximising views to the park from the street. While the dynamic, sculptural language of the building highlights its identity as a cultural landmark, distinguishing it from adjacent commercial and residential buildings, the pavilion's form reflects its function as a bridge between this urban fabric and the canal. The main exhibition hall is a spectacular open space interrupted only by the two angled cores that rise through the building. Accessed by an open, sculptural staircase leading up from the public area below, it provides flexibility of use while maintaining a strong and unique formal identity through the folding of walls and roof. Glazing is kept to a minimum in order to reduce solar gain and control light levels, with natural light and ventilation provided by clerestory windows and a single large window to the south offering uninterrupted views across the Biennale Park. A smaller, multi-purpose mezzanine floor leads to the gently undulating roof, an amphitheatre space for outdoor events offering views across the cultural quarter to the sea. Below the main body of the pavilion, a basement level for offices, retail, flexible studio spaces or classrooms and services, is partially sunk into the terrain below the pavilion. A courtyard provides light and independent access for staff, accessible from both street level and the canal side. The roof of the retail units forms a terrace shaded by the cantilevered pavilion. Overlooking the canal, this allows the ground floor of the building to extend out into the landscape, reinforcing the connection between the pavilion and its surroundings.

Mit der Gestaltung dieses Kunstpavillons soll das Potenzial des Areals bestmöglich genutzt werden. Hierfür wird eine dynamische Verbindung zwischen dem urbanen Geflecht des neuen Kulturdistrikts und dem Kanal im Zentrum des Biennale Parks geschaffen. Der Hauptausstellungsraum liegt über dem Park und öffnet so seinen Erdgeschossbereich der Öffentlichkeit. Dieser Raum ist mehr als nur ein Tor zu dem Ausstellungsraum oder eine alternative Verbindung zwischen Straße und Kanal. Er ist ein Ort, den neugierige Passanten erkunden können, und zugleich eine Bühne für kleine Veranstaltungen oder Vorführungen. Die Wände, die den Ausstellungsraum darüber umschließen, kragen weit aus, spenden angenehmen Schatten für die Park- und Pavillonbesucher und erlauben so auch von der Straße aus einen guten Blick in den Park. Während die dynamische, skulpturale Form des Gebäudes dessen Identität als weithin sichtbare kulturelle Einrichtung erkennbar werden lässt und es von den angrenzenden Gewerbe- und Wohnbauten absetzt, spiegelt sich in der Form auch dessen Funktion als Brücke zwischen den angrenzenden urbanen Strukturen und dem Kanal wider. Die Hauptausstellungshalle ist ein spektakulärer offener Raum, der nur von zwei schrägen Kernen, die sich durch das Gebäude ziehen, unterbrochen wird. Vom öffentlichen Bereich gelangt man über einen offenen, plastisch geformten Treppenaufgang nach oben in einen Raum, der flexibel zu nutzen ist und durch die gefalteten Wand- und Dachflächen und seine einzigartige Form dennoch eine ausgeprägte Identität besitzt. Um die Aufheizung des Gebäudes durch Sonneneinstrahlung möglichst gering zu halten, sind die Glasflächen auf ein Minimum reduziert. Tageslicht und Luft gelangen durch Oberlichter und ein einziges großes Fenster an der Südseite, das einen freien Blick auf den Biennale Park bietet, nach innen. Ein etwas kleineres, für verschiedene Zwecke nutzbares Mezzaningeschoss führt auf das leicht gewellte Dach mit einem Amphitheater für Außenveranstaltungen und mit Blick über die gesamte Insel zum Meer. Unter dem Gebäude im Souterrainbereich befinden sich Büros, Geschäfte, frei nutzbare Räume für Ateliers oder Schulklassen sowie Versorgungsräume. Sie erhalten Licht über einen Innenhof, der auch als separater Eingang für die Mitarbeiter sowohl von der Straße als auch von der Kanalseite dient. Das Dach der Geschäfte wird zu einer Terrasse, die von dem auskragenden Pavillon verschattet wird. Mit Blick auf den Kanal setzt sich so das Erdgeschoss in die Landschaft fort und verstärkt die Verbindung des Pavillons mit seiner Umgebung.

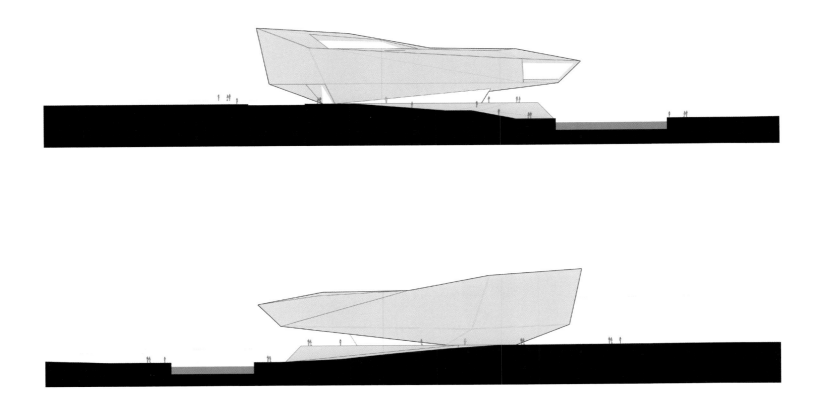

OMA

City in the Desert / Ras Al Khaimah
Rak Jebel Al Jais Mountain Resort / Ras Al Khaimah
Waterfront City / Dubai

~ A leading international design studio practising architecture, urbanism and cultural analysis, OMA's buildings and masterplans around the world insist on intelligent forms while inventing new possibilities for content and everyday use. OMA is led by seven partners – Rem Koolhaas, Ellen van Loon, Reinier de Graaf, Shohei Shigematsu, Iyad Alsaka, David Gianotten and Victor van der Chijs – and sustains an international presence with offices in Rotterdam, New York, Beijing and Hong Kong. The work of OMA has won several prestigious international awards including the Pritzker Architecture Prize (2000), the Praemium Imperiale (Japan, 2003), the RIBA Gold Medal (UK, 2004), the Mies van der Rohe European Union Prize for Contemporary Architecture (2005) and the Golden Lion for Lifetime Achievement at the Venice Biennale (2010).

~ Als eines der führenden internationalen Büros für Architektur, Stadtplanung und Kulturanalysen verbindet OMA in seinen Gebäuden und Masterplänen weltweit intelligente Formen mit neuen Inhalten und Alltagstauglichkeit. OMA wird von sieben Partnern geleitet – Rem Koolhaas, Ellen van Loon, Reinier de Graaf, Shohei Shigematsu, Iyad Alsaka, David Gianotten und Victor van der Chijs – und unterhält Büros in Rotterdam, New York, Peking und Hongkong. Die Arbeiten von OMA wurden mit vielen wichtigen internationalen Preisen ausgezeichnet, darunter der Pritzker Architecture Prize (2000), der Praemium Imperiale (Japan, 2003), die RIBA Gold Medal (GB, 2004), der Mies van der Rohe European Union Prize for Contemporary Architecture (2005) und der Goldene Löwe für das Lebenswerk auf der Architektur-Biennale in Venedig (2010).

~ CITY IN THE DESERT
Gross Floor Area: 994,600 m^2
Total Site Area: 1,204,200 m^2
150,000 inhabitants
Ongoing

For some time now desert developments have been constructed as though they have been created for anywhere. Large sections of the desert are being turned into high-maintenance green lawns. Levels of energy and water consumption are representing immense ecological cost. Even with pressures to join the development race in the UAE, many areas of the country still feel relatively virgin. Not yet "developed" to the level of Dubai or Abu Dhabi, these areas could still avoid the type of rampant global modernism that has hit other parts of the UAE, and opt for a more considered approach. With 43 km^2 for 150,000 new inhabitants, the plan for the City in the Desert represents a quantum leap in the region's development. Its sheer size almost automatically implies that choices made in relation to the Gateway Plan will turn out to be choices for the region as a whole. The project marks a decisive moment in the course of the region's future planning. How does one create a welcoming city in an unwelcoming climate? The fort is one of the city's most authentic and compelling solutions; the most efficient and compact form of urbanisation, where work and living form an integrated whole. This scheme combines the conveniences of one's home with the proximity of cultural and social provisions, the intimacy of the traditional street with smooth accessibility and quality public realm with a large quantum of development. Concentration, density and synergy are the main features, not born out of nostalgia, but of absolute necessity.

Eine ganze Zeit lang wurden Bauprojekte in der Wüste ohne Rücksicht auf ihre Umgebung konzipiert. Großflächige Wüstenabschnitte wurden in pflegeaufwendige grüne Wiesen verwandelt. Der hohe Verbrauch von Strom und Wasser bedeutet immense ökologische Kosten. Obwohl der Entwicklungsdruck in den VAE groß ist, gibt es dort noch viele relativ jungfräuliche Gebiete. In Gegenden, die nicht so „entwickelt" sind wie Dubai oder Abu Dhabi, könnte die ungezügelte Modernisierung durch umsichtige Planung vermieden werden. Mit 43 km^2 für 150.000 neue Einwohner stellt die Planung für die „City in the Desert" einen Quantensprung in der Entwicklung der Region dar. Allein durch seine Größe wird schon klar, dass Entscheidungen, die dieses Projekt betreffen, Entscheidungen für die ganze Region sind. Die Planung orientiert sich an folgender Frage: Wie erschafft man eine einladende Stadt in einem unwirtlichen Klima? Das Fort ist dafür eine authentische, sich fast aufzwingende Lösung. Es ist die effizienteste und kompakteste Form der Urbanisierung, in der Leben und Arbeiten an einem Ort integriert sind. Das Konzept verbindet die Annehmlichkeiten des eigenen Zuhauses mit leicht erreichbaren sozialen und kulturellen Einrichtungen, die Intimität einer traditionellen Straße mit guter Zugänglichkeit und einen angenehmen öffentlichen Raum mit mannigfaltigen Möglichkeiten der Entwicklung. Konzentration, Dichte und Synergie sind die wichtigsten Merkmale des Entwurfs, konzipiert nicht aus Nostalgie, sondern aus absoluter Notwendigkeit heraus.

The Units

~ RAK JEBEL AL JAIS MOUNTAIN RESORT
Ongoing

The mountain resort of Ras Al Khaimah presents a spectacular natural setting. Rather than domesticating the barren slopes into the standard environment of the traditional tourist resort, this project aims to create a destination that exploits the true natural conditions. A path with implemented villas deliberately navigates the mountain. Development clings to the path while most of the site remains untouched, preserving the mountain's natural integrity. The villas articulate the trajectory of the resort. Specific moments along the path, chosen for the unique topography, interrupt the line of villas. These include The Units – like a pixelated carpet over the landscape, the modular units form a geometric abstraction of the natural terrain. Sited in a moderate to steep area, dwellings step down the mountain to create a series of connected roof terraces; The Dam – its curving arc spanning across a valley, its roof doubling as a road to form an integral part of the path. Filled with apartment and hotel units, The Dam continues the surrounding rock walls of the valley; The Wedge – like an extension of the mountain, this appears from street level as an inclined plane projecting out over the valley and serving as a public plaza that can be programmed with a variety of activities. Below, a ramping circuit descends through the building, connecting the plaza to a hotel, apartments, community centre, commercial areas and a cable car terminus; The Bridge – by connecting two high points separated by a gully, this creates a shortcut. Forming a secondary path, the middle level of the building is an outdoor area that functions as the entrance for all levels.

Das hochgelegene Urlaubsresort Ras al-Khaima bietet ein spektakuläres natürliches Umfeld. Anstatt die kargen Hänge zu domestizieren, wie man es von den traditionellen Touristenorten gewohnt ist, will dieses Projekt ein Reiseziel sein, das den natürlichen landschaftlichen Gegebenheiten angepasst ist. Ein schmaler Pfad mit angrenzenden Villen windet sich den Berg entlang. Nur im Bereich dieses Weges wird das Gebäude erschlossen, der Rest der Bergfläche bleibt unberührt. Die Villen bilden eine Art Umrissplan für den Ort. An manchen Stellen wird ihre Reihe unterbrochen, um die einzigartige Topographie wirken zu lassen. Zu den Bauten entlang des Weges gehören unter anderem The Units, die sich wie eine Art Flickenteppich über die Landschaft legen und das natürliche Terrain in einer geometrischen Abstraktion nachbilden. Die an einem leicht abfallenden Hang gelegenen Wohngebäude folgen Erhebungen und bilden teilweise zusammenhängende Dachterrassen. The Dam ist ein Staudamm, der sich über ein Tal spannt und dessen obere Kante als Straße den Erschließungsweg des Geländes fortsetzt. Der Damm, der sich elegant in die Felswände des Tals einfügt, beherbergt in seinem Inneren Wohn- und Hoteleinheiten. The Wedge wirkt wie eine Erweiterung des Berges; von der Straße her wirkt dieser Keil wie ein Flugzeug, das sich gerade über das Tal erhebt. Sein Dach dient als öffentlicher Platz, der sich für diverse Aktivitäten eignet. Durch das Gebäude führt eine Art absteigender Schneckengang zu einem Hotel, zu Wohnungen, einem Gemeinschaftshaus, zu Geschäften und einer Straßenbahnhaltestelle. The Bridge schließlich überbrückt eine Schlucht und wird so zur Abkürzung auf einem zweiten Weg. Dabei ist die mittlere Ebene des Bauwerks ein Freiluftbereich, der als Eingang für die anderen Ebenen dient.

The Dam

The Wedge

The Bridge

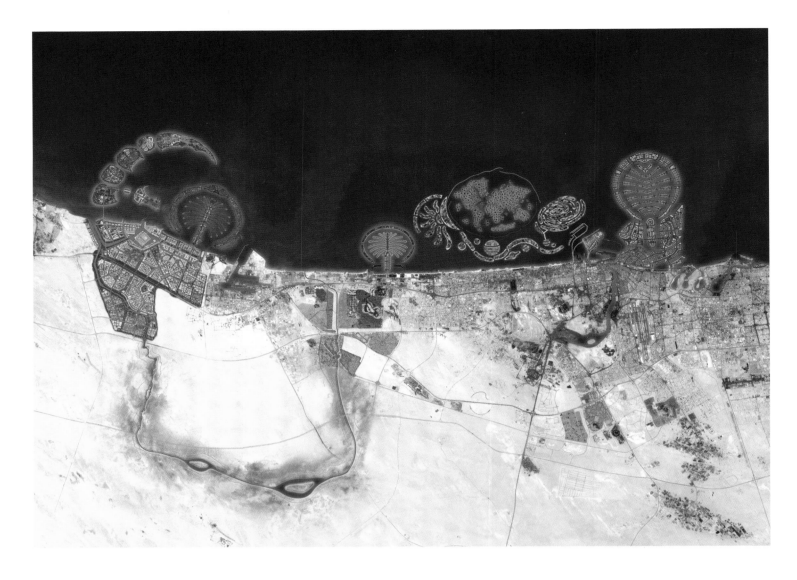

~ WATERFRONT CITY
Mixed-use Masterplan
Total Floor Area: 11.8 million m²
Island Size: 1,310 m x 1,310 m
Ongoing

Waterfront City in Dubai is a masterplan of unprecedented scale and ambition, aiming to generate density and diversity in a city that has seen explosive growth in recent years but little cultivation of street-level urban activity that most metropolises thrive on. The development consists of an artificial island linked to four distinct neighbourhoods – Madinat Al Soor, the Boulevard, the Marina, and the Resorts – which together are twice the size of Hong Kong Island and yield a total floor space of 11.8 million m². The design takes an optimistic view of the future of urbanism and exploits two usually opposing elements of 21st-century architecture: the generic and the iconic. The island is divided into 25 traditional city blocks that permit a rational, repeatable and exponential urbanism redolent of Manhattan. An equal distribution of residential and office space stimulates a natural flow of street life night and day. The highest towers are strategically clustered along the southern edge to provide maximum protection for the Island against the desert sun. The island connects to the mainland by bridges on each side of its square, fusing with Dubai's monorail system. Along the southern and eastern periphery of Waterfront City a ring road deflects passing traffic, and is lined by a protective arc of buildings overlooking the water and enclosing a mixed-use area.

Waterfront City in Dubai ist ein überaus ehrgeiziger Masterplan von beispiellosen Dimensionen. Sein Ziel ist es, Verdichtung und Diversität in einer Stadt zu schaffen, die seit einigen Jahren ein riesiges Wachstum prägt, während die Aktivierung der Straßenebene, vernachlässigt wurde. Das Projekt besteht aus einer künstlichen Insel, die mit vier verschiedenen Vierteln verbunden ist: Madinat Al Soor, dem Boulevard, der Marina und den Erholungsorten. Alle zusammen sind zweimal so groß wie Hong Kong Island und erstrecken sich über 11,8 Millionen m². Der Entwurf beruht auf einer optimistischen Sicht auf die urbane Zukunft und stützt sich auf zwei, zumeist gegensätzliche Elemente der Architektur des 21. Jahrhunderts: das Generische und das Herausragende. Die Insel ist in 25 klassische Straßenblocks aufgeteilt, die einen rationalen, reproduzierbaren und exponentiellen Städtebau ermöglichen, der stark an Manhattan erinnert. Wohn- und Büroraum sollen zu gleichen Teilen auf die Gebäude verteilt werden. Dadurch werden die Straßen sowohl tagsüber als auch nachts belebt sein. Die höchsten Türme werden um den südlichen Rand gruppiert, um die Insel bestmöglich gegen die Wüstensonne abzuschirmen. Von der Insel führen Brücken zum Festland, die in das Netz der Dubaier Einschienenbahn eingebunden sind. An der südlichen und östlichen Peripherie von Waterfront City nimmt eine Umgehungsstraße den Durchgangsverkehr auf. Sie wird gesäumt von einem Schutzwall aus Gebäuden mit Blick auf das Wasser.

ONL

Manhal Oasis / Abu Dhabi
Al Nasser Group Corporate Headquarters / Abu Dhabi
Abu Dhabi Automotive Complex / Abu Dhabi

~ Architect Kas Oosterhuis and visual artist Ilona Lénárd are directors of the multidisciplinary design office Oosterhuis_Lénárd – where architects, visual artists, web designers and programmers collaborate to practise the fusion of art and architecture and technique on a digital platform. An office where reality and virtuality meet – ONL has developed a state-of-the-art design process called File-to-Factory (F2F) – which can realise a true design-and-build development. With the help of new programming techniques, ONL controls the complex geometry and engineering of double-curved surfaces and supportive construction – a new approach to parametric architectural and constructive detailing.

~ Der Architekt Kas Oosterhuis und die bildende Künstlerin Ilona Lénárd leiten das interdisziplinäre Designbüro Oosterhuis_Lénárd. Dort arbeiten Architekten, Künstler, Web-Designer und Programmierer gemeinsam daran, Kunst, Architektur und Technik auf einer digitalen Plattform miteinander zu verschmelzen. Realität und Virtualität treffen hier aufeinander. Mit File-to-Factory (F2F) hat ONL einen hochmodernen Gestaltungsprozess entwickelt, mit dem ein Bauprojekt von der Planung bis zur Umsetzung begleitet werden kann. Mittels neuester Software berechnet ONL die komplexe Geometrie doppelt gekrümmter Flächen und die dafür notwendigen tragenden Konstruktionen. Das ist eine neue Herangehensweise an parametrische Architektur und ihrer konstruktiven Umsetzung.

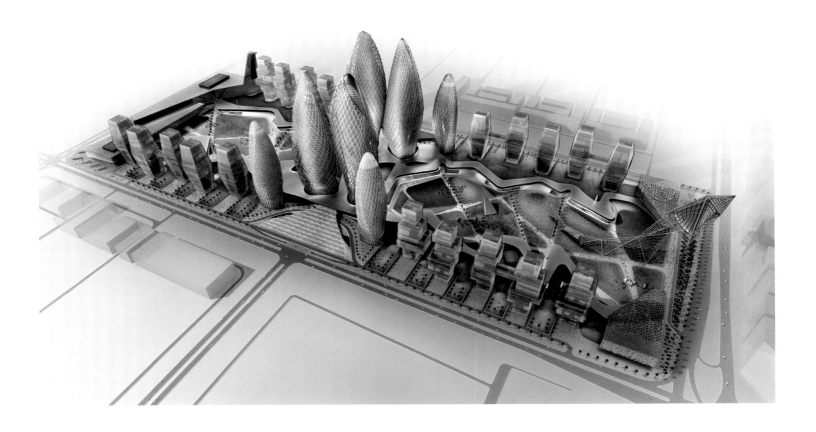

~ MANHAL OASIS
Masterplan for the Al Manhal Palace site
Client: International Capital Trading LLC
Gross Floor Area: 2,000,000 m²
50,000 inhabitants
Ongoing

The Manhal Oasis masterplan in Abu Dhabi has the ambition to be a destination town with three major attractors: the cultural gate from Airport Road to the Manhal Oasis, featuring two museums and the Manhal Xperience attraction; the gate at the southeast side, featuring the Future Fit shopping mall and wellness centre; and the Manhal Downtown and Manhal Souks inside the four 60-storey high twisted towers. The gates lead to a large urban oasis where precious trees nurtured by the late Sheikh Zayed, former ruler and owner of the Manhal Palace, would be relocated from the Manhal plantation. Beyond the canyons are four 30-storey mixed-use towers, nodding to the desert mountains in the distance. The development represents the seven Emirates: the central buildings being Abu Dhabi, the souk area representing Dubai, the cultural areas Sharjah, the ponds for Ajman and Umm Al Quwain, the side buildings symbolising the mountains of Ras Al Khaimah and the green area representing Fujairah. The project has the challenging aim of preserving as much as possible of the existing plantation and parkland, while adding over 2 million m² of urban development to create a new destination for local, regional and international users and visitors.

Ziel des Masterplans für die Manhal-Oase in Abu Dhabi ist es, zu einem Ausflugsziel zu werden. Drei Hauptattraktionen sollen die Menschen anziehen: die Kulturpforte, die von der Airport Road zur Manhal-Oase führt und mit zwei Museen und der Manhal Xperience aufwartet; die Südost-Pforte, die eine Einkaufspassage und ein Wellness-Center aufbietet; und schließlich Manhal Downtown und die Manhal-Suks im Inneren der vier 60 Stockwerke hohen, gedrehten Türme. Die Pforten führen zu einer großen Stadtoase, in der kostbare Bäume stehen, die Scheich Zayed, der verstorbene Emir von Abu Dhabi und Eigentümer des Manhal-Palastes, selbst gepflegt hat. Jenseits der Schluchten befinden sich vier 30-geschossige Türme mit Mischnutzung, die Wüstenbergen in der Ferne zugewandt sind. Das Konzept repräsentiert die sieben Emirate: Das zentrale Gebäude steht für Abu Dhabi, die Suk-Fläche repräsentiert Dubai, die kulturellen Bereiche stehen für Sharja, die Teiche für Ajman und Umm al-Kawain, die Gebäude an der Seite symbolisieren die Berge von Ras al-Khaima und die grüne Zone repräsentiert Fujaira. Das Projekt hat das anspruchsvolle Ziel, so viel wie möglich von der existierenden Bepflanzung und der Parklandschaft zu erhalten und gleichzeitig mehr als 2 Mio. m² neugebauter Fläche zur Verfügung zu stellen, um ein Reiseziel für örtliche, regionale und internationale Besucher zu erschaffen.

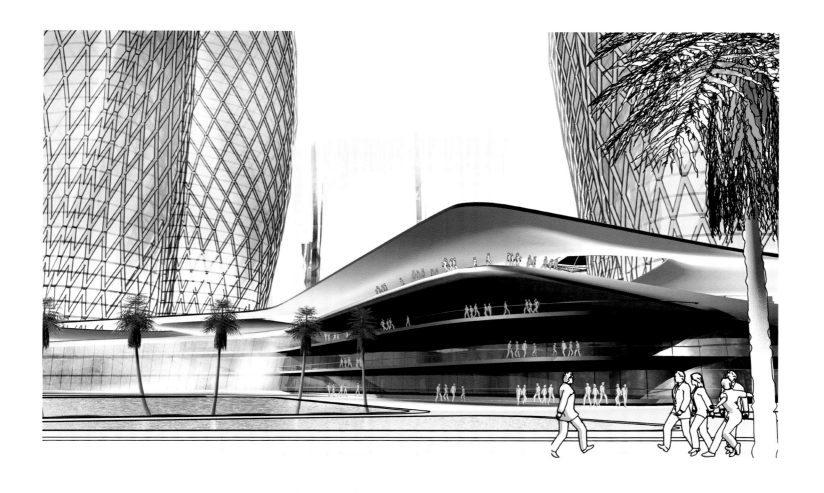

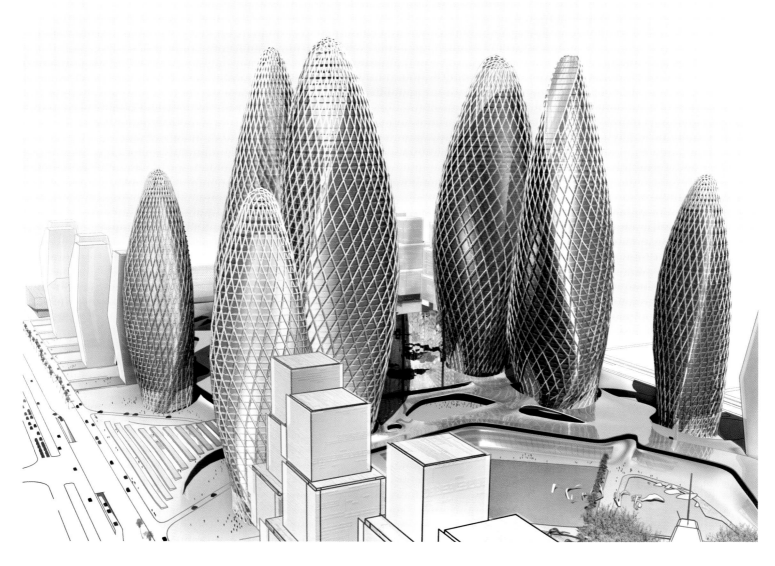

~ AL NASSER GROUP CORPORATE HEADQUARTERS
Client: Al Nasser Investments
Project & Development Manager: Northcroft Middle East
Gross Floor Area: 21,604 m²
Materials: steel, aluminium, glass
Under construction

Despite strict design constraints, ONL has found a solution which combines iconic architecture with a functional layout. This integrated approach forms the basis for cost-effective architectural eloquence. The architectural team developed a vase-shaped tower, narrow at the base, gaining volume in the shaft and tapered towards the top, styled by subtly slicing and chamfering the otherwise rectangular floor plan. Relatively modest interventions and parametric modifications of the rectangular shape while retaining the structural integrity of the design create the tower's distinctive form. Its shape improves sustainability in respect to wind loads, as the corners of the floor plan are rounded off. The façade is completely covered with glass – with around 25% vision glass and 75% contrast coloured spandrel panels. The structural glazing technique guarantees minimal concentration of moist dust grains, setting a sound basis for low maintenance costs. All office space is no deeper than 6 m, allowing workers to benefit from direct daylight, so saving on lighting costs. All materials are mass-customised – offering high levels of sustainability compared to traditional mass-production methods. The load-bearing structural façade needs no separate support structure for its cladding system – as both use the same tessellation. ONL's innovative façade system reduces working hours, time and money, and is naturally sustainable due to its straightforward, no-nonsense approach.

Trotz strenger Gestaltungsvorgaben fand ONL eine Lösung, die unkonventionelle Architektur mit bewährter Funktionalität verbindet. Diese integrierte Herangehensweise ist die Grundlage für eine kostengünstige architektonische Vielsprachigkeit. Das Architektenteam hat einen vasenförmigen Turm entworfen. Er ist schmal an der Basis, gewinnt mit zunehmender Höhe an Volumen und verjüngt sich zur Spitze hin wieder. Der an sich rechtwinklige Grundriss wurde subtil aufgeschnitten und abgekantet. Relativ bescheidene Eingriffe und parametrische Modifikationen des Rechtecks geben dem Turm seine ungewöhnliche Form, ohne die Tragfähigkeit zu beeinträchtigen. Die abgerundeten Ecken des Gebäudes bieten auch dem Wind weniger Angriffsfläche. Die Fassade ist komplett in Glas gehüllt – rund 25 % davon Sichtglas und 75 % gefärbte Brüstungsplatten. Die lasttragende Verglasung hält Feuchtigkeits- und Staubrückstände minimal und die Wartungskosten gering. Kein Büro ist tiefer als 6 m. So kann jeder Angestellte bei Tageslicht arbeiten und man spart Stromkosten. Die Materialien sind per individualisierter Massenfertigung hergestellt. Das macht sie nachhaltiger als bei klassischer Massenproduktion. Die tragende Glasfassade muss nicht zusätzlich gestützt werden, denn die vorgehängten Paneele sind im gleichen Muster angebracht wie das Tragwerk der Fassade. Das innovative Fassadensystem von ONL verringert die Zahl der benötigten Arbeitsstunden und ist aufgrund seiner konsequenten Ausgestaltung relativ langlebig.

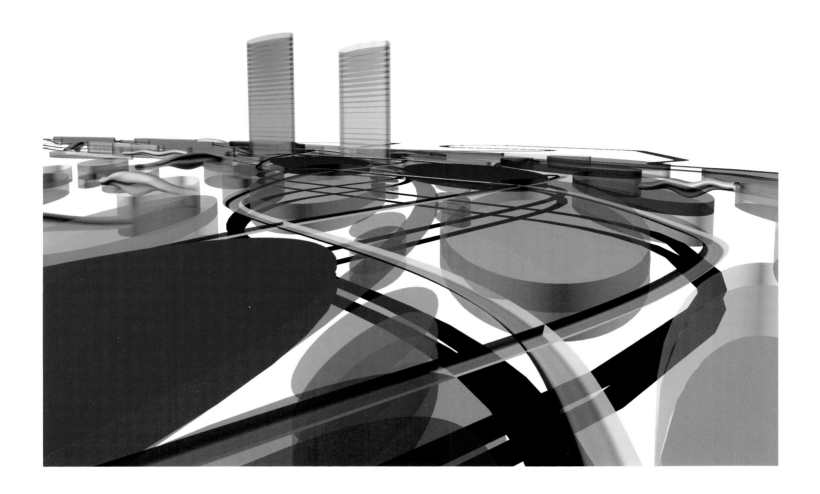

~ ABU DHABI AUTOMOTIVE COMPLEX
Masterplan for large automotive complex
Client: Aldar Properties Abu Dhabi
Gross Floor Area: 1,000,000 m²
Length: 2.5 km
Ongoing

The masterplan for the Abu Dhabi Automotive Complex covers a site of more than 6 km² at the crossing between the Abu Dhabi–Dubai highway and Airport Road. A 2.5 km terminal building features various satellite spaces to represent different motor brands. The major brands will have showrooms and garages for maintenance and services, selling both used and new car models. Car parts shops and garages, ranging from car tyres to the complete tuning and customising of cars, will add to the overall excitement of driving, watching, playing and living with cars. However, to attract a sufficiently wide audience, various other elements have been added to the mix – including a motor museum, styling centre, design academy and children's car track, alongside more general retail facilities for fashion, interior design and electronics and several themed food courts. A hotel, conference centre and offices will support special events. While the core business is offering high-level service to car customers, at the same time the complex offers attractions for those with a general interest in new developments in car design and engineering.

Der Masterplan für den Automotive Complex von Abu Dhabi bedeckt eine Fläche von über 6 km², die an der Kreuzung des Abu Dhabi-Dubai Highways und der Airport Road liegt. Das 2,5 km lange Gebäude bietet Präsentationsflächen für die verschiedensten Automarken auf. Für die größten Hersteller sind eigene Showrooms und Reparaturwerkstätten vorgesehen, in denen neue und gebrauchte Wagen verkauft werden. Werkstätten und Geschäfte für Autoteile, die von Reifen bis zum Tuning und zur Sonderausstattung alles anbieten, verstärken die Atmosphäre des automobilen Lebens. Um ein breites Publikum anzusprechen, wurden noch verschiedene andere Bereiche eingerichtet, darunter ein Automuseum, ein Styling Center, eine Design-Akademie und eine Kinderrennbahn. Dazu kommen noch der allgemeine Einzelhandel mit Mode-, Einrichtungs- und Elektronikgeschäften sowie diverse Gastronomiebereiche. Ein Hotel, ein Konferenzzentrum und Büros stehen für Veranstaltungen zur Verfügung. Während sich das Hauptangebot an Kunden richtet, die hohen Service rund ums Auto erwarten, ist der Komplex durch das zusätzliche Angebot auch für Menschen attraktiv, die sich für die neuesten Entwicklungen auf dem Gebiet von Automobiltechnik und -design interessieren.

QUANTUM-AIP

Arabian Film Institute Complex / Dubai
Executive Waterfront Residential Island Complex / Dubai
Bio Research and Development Institute / Dubai
Corniche Museum and Hospitality Complex / Abu Dhabi

~ Quantum-AIP is an architectural, planning and interior design studio which provides a wide range of design services focusing on liveable and sustainable environments. Founded by Behr Champana and Howard Chen, they have over 40 years of joint experience and are renowned for mentoring a culture of creativity and productivity devoid of any age-old assumptions. A particular characteristic of the firm's design approach is its collaborative process through its specialised think tank and visioning studios. With experience in the US, Caribbean, Latin America and Europe, over the last 10 years the company has expanded its design expertise into the emerging markets – specifically the Middle East, South Asia and the Far East.

~ Quantum-AIP ist ein Büro, dessen Schwerpunkte auf Architektur, Planung und Innenarchitektur liegen und das Gestaltungslösungen für eine lebenswerte und nachhaltige Umwelt bietet. Die Gründer Behr Champana und Howard Chen besitzen gemeinsam über 40 Jahre Erfahrung und stehen für eine von festgefahrenen Vorstellungen losgelöste Kultur der Kreativität und Produktivität. Das Besondere ihres Ansatzes ist der kollaborative Prozess, den die Entwürfe in der Denkfabrik und den Ateliers von Quantum-AIP durchlaufen. In den vergangenen zehn Jahren konnte das Büro Erfahrungen in den USA, der Karibik, in Lateinamerika und Europa sammeln und öffnet sich damit nun auch aufstrebenden Märkten insbesondere im Nahen Osten, im südasiatischen Raum und im Fernen Osten.

~ ARABIAN FILM INSTITUTE COMPLEX
Ongoing

The key aims of the Arabian Film Institute Complex are to preserve the Middle East's vanishing film heritage and to train future filmmakers. Strengthened by the surge of film festivals in the region, the Institute also serves as a platform to bring together leading artists, educators and young talent. This state-of-the-art complex – whose design has been inspired by the traditional movie reels – will include an IMAX, a large performance hall, ten screen theatres, flexible and permanent exhibition spaces, a film library, and themed restaurants. The façade itself can be a projection screen for outdoor film screenings, promotions and concerts.

Die Hauptziele des Arabian Film Institute Complex sind die Erhaltung des immer weiter zurückgedrängten Filmerbes des Nahen Ostens und die Ausbildung zukünftiger Filmemacher. Unterstützt durch eine Reihe von Filmfestivals in der Region, dient das Institute auch als Plattform, die führende Künstler, Filmpädagogen und junge Talente zusammenbringt. Zu dem modernen Komplex, dessen Gestaltung von den traditionellen Filmrollen inspiriert ist, gehören ein IMAX-Kino, ein großer Veranstaltungssaal, ausgestattet mit modernster Elektronik, Hydraulik und Bühnentechnik, zehn Kinos, flexible Ausstellungsräume für Dauer- und Sonderausstellungen, eine Filmbibliothek und ein Museum sowie Geschäfte und Restaurants. Die Fassade selbst kann als Projektionsfläche für Filmvorführungen, Konzerte und Werbung genutzt werden.

~ EXECUTIVE WATERFRONT RESIDENTIAL ISLAND COMPLEX
Ongoing

This project incorporates five high-end housing "pods" for a man-made residential island, each containing 15 apartments. The architectural language for this residential prototype takes inspiration from an eroded sea shell and the luxurious residential facility incorporates the latest technology systems to facilitate personalised concierge services and resort amenities. While the island residents will share community amenities, clubhouse and marina, each unit will have its own outdoor entertainment area, complete with an indoor/outdoor lap pool off the main living rooms.

Das Projekt besteht aus fünf hochmodernen „Kapseln" mit jeweils 15 Wohnungen auf einer künstlichen Wohninsel. Die Gestaltungssprache für diesen Wohn-Prototyp ist inspiriert von einer ausgewaschenen Meeresmuschel. Die Luxuswohnanlage besitzt die modernsten Technologien, die individuelle Dienstleistungen und weitere Annehmlichkeiten ermöglichen. Als Gemeinschaftseinrichtungen gibt es unter anderem ein Clubhaus und eine Marina, darüber hinaus besitzt jede Wohneinheit ihren eigenen Außenbereich mit Innen-/Außenpool vor den Wohnräumen.

~ BIO RESEARCH AND DEVELOPMENT INSTITUTE
Ongoing

The Institute will be conducting advanced biological research on genetics and molecular biology, neurosciences, plant biology, and population science to gain new understanding and potential new therapies to treat fatal diseases, brain abnormalities and birth defects, as well as improving the future quality and availability of the world's food supply. Designed to be a highly secured facility, the architectural form and site plan is an abstracted visual representation of the human hand skin cells. The building will also feature a conference centre, dormitories and gymnasium.

Das Institut ist spezialisiert auf Genforschung, Molekularbiologie, Neurowissenschaften, Botanik und Bevölkerungsforschung, um mit neuen Erkenntnissen Therapien zur Behandlung schwerer Erkrankungen von Anomalitäten des Gehirns und von Geburtsfehlern zu entwickeln. Darüber hinaus arbeitet das Institut an einer Verbesserung der Qualität und Verfügbarkeit von Lebensmitteln. Das Gebäude bietet ein Höchstmaß an Sicherheit. Seine Form sowie die Gesamtanlage sind eine abstrahierte Darstellung der Hautzellen der menschlichen Hand. Ein Konferenzzentrum, ein Gästehaus und eine Sporthalle komplettieren die Einrichtung.

~ CORNICHE MUSEUM AND HOSPITALITY COMPLEX
Ongoing

The strategic location of this waterfront project required a 150-room hotel within a flexible venue that could also provide exhibition or public conference facilities. With its dual function, each component requires its own visual identity – thus the intersecting, double boomerang design provides access, circulation and separation of use, while creating a distinctive, yet unified building structure.

Das Bauprogramm für dieses ufernahe Gebäude fordert ein Hotel mit 150 Zimmern innerhalb einer flexiblen Anlage, in der auch Ausstellungen und Konferenzen durchgeführt werden können. Jeder Funktion ist ein Baukörper mit eigener Identität zugeordnet. Die beiden jeweils wie ein Bumerang geformten Gebäude besitzen einen gemeinsamen Bereich mit Zu- und Aufgängen, der die Nutzungen voneinander trennt und trotzdem ein einheitliches Ganzes entstehen lässt.

REISER + UMEMOTO

O-14 / Dubai
Aeon / Dubai

~ Jesse Reiser and Nanako Umemoto founded Reiser + Umemoto in New York in 1986. The internationally renowned architectural practice has projects of varying scales – spanning infrastructure, landscape design, residential and commercial buildings and furniture designs. Reiser is currently an Associate Professor of Architecture at Princeton University. Reiser + Umemoto gained considerable international attention after being awarded first place honours during the international jury phase of the Shenzhen Airport Competition. In 2008, the firm was awarded the Presidential Citation of the Cooper Union for outstanding practical and theoretical contributions to the field of architecture. More recently, it has won the Taipei Pop Music Centre Competition.

~ Jesse Reiser und Nanako Umemoto gründeten 1986 in New York Reiser + Umemoto. Das international hoch angesehene Architekturbüro plant Projekte unterschiedlicher Größe – Infrastruktur- und Landschaftsbau, Wohn- und Gewerbebauten sowie Möbel. Reiser ist derzeit Associate Professor für Architektur an der Princeton University. Reiser + Umemoto wurden international bekannt, nachdem eine internationale Jury ihrem Entwurf beim Wettbewerb für den Shenzhen Airport in die engere Auswahl genommen hatte. 2008 wurde das Büro mit der Presidential Citation of the Cooper Union für außergewöhnliche praktische und theoretische Beiträge im Bereich Architektur ausgezeichnet. Vor kurzem gewannen sie den Wettbewerb für das Taipei Pop Music Centre.

~ O-14
Client: Creekside Development Corporation, Dubai, UAE
Site Area: 3,195 m²
Gross Floor Area: 15,979 m²
Building Area: 27,870 m²
Structure: perforated concrete exoskeleton
Height: 105.7 m
Storeys: 22
Completion: 2010

The O-14 building occupies a prominent location on the waterfront of Dubai Creek in Dubai's Business Bay district. The office tower typology has effectively been turned inside out: structure and skin have been flipped to offer a new economy of tectonics and space. The concrete shell provides an efficient structural exoskeleton that frees the core from the burden of lateral forces, so creating highly efficient, column-free open spaces in the building's interior. The exoskeleton of O-14 becomes the primary vertical and lateral structure for the building, allowing the column-free office floors to span between it and the minimal core. Tenants can accordingly arrange the flexible floor space according to individual needs. By moving the lateral bracing for the building to the perimeter, the core, which is traditionally enlarged to receive lateral loading in most curtain wall office towers, can be minimised for vertical loading, utilities and circulation. The main shell is organised as a diagrid which allows for arbitrary openings while maintaining a structural integrity, adding and subtracting material where required. This module allows for variations in the façade to create striking visual and atmospheric effects without changing the basic structural form.

Das O-14 steht an einem exponierten Ort am Ufer des Dubai Creek in der Business Bay von Dubai. Die Büroturm-Typologie wurde von innen nach außen gewendet: Hülle und tragende Strukturen wurden umgedreht, um neue statische und räumliche Möglichkeiten zu schaffen. Die Betonhülle ist ein wirkungsvolles Außenskelett, das verhindert, dass seitliche Kräfte auf den Kern wirken. Im Inneren des Gebäudes entstehen so hocheffiziente, stützenlose offene Räume. Das Außenskelett von O-14 wird zum vertikalen und horizontalen Haupttragwerk des Gebäudes. Dadurch können sich die stützenfreien Büroetagen zwischen der Hülle und dem verdichteten Kern aufspannen und die Büroflächen ganz nach den Anforderungen der Mieter aufgeteilt werden. Durch das Verlegen der Seitenstütze nach außen konnte der Kern, der bei den meisten Bürotürmen mit Vorhangfassade üblicherweise vergrößert ist, um die Seitenkräfte aufzunehmen, minimiert werden. Er muss nur noch die vertikalen Lasten tragen und die Versorgungs- und Lüftungsschächte aufnehmen. Die Außenhülle besteht aus einer Art überdimensioniertem Stützgewebe, das willkürlich angeordnete Öffnungen zulässt, ohne etwas von ihrer Tragkraft einzubüßen. Wo es gewünscht wird, kann Material hinzugefügt oder weggenommen werden. So können in der Fassade auffallende visuelle und atmosphärische Variationen entstehen.

~ AEON
Total Built-up Area: 58,806 m²
Storeys: 45
Ongoing

Aeon's prominent L-shaped location in Dubai's Jumeirah Lakes district, amidst a backdrop of densely spaced towers, offered a welcome opportunity to rethink the tower typology in context. The shape of the site was the catalyst for the design to be horizontal rather than vertical. Dubai's predilection for curtain wall clad towers was cast aside in favour of a responsive cladding system more in tune with the arid desert environment. The building's folded plan-form combines the inherent efficiency of parallel floor slabs with rich, sculptural possibilities, with the new floor-plate allowing for more individual, small to mid-size office configurations. The design creates a new concept for the building skin: replacing the typical curtain wall solution, a floor-to-ceiling window-wall assembly creates the building's folded forms with a perforated aluminium panel skin providing aesthetic and environmental benefits – shading the building from glare and heat, while allowing for directed views from within – created in the tips of the folds, resulting in more corner offices. The rich quality and variation of the outer fabric is created by following its folded building form, and while the built element is standard, the openings are unique and vary continuously.

Das an markanter Stelle gelegene L-förmige Grundstück von Aeon im Dubaier Viertel Jumeirah Lakes bot die willkommene Gelegenheit, die Typologie des Turms im Kontext seiner Umgebung neu zu denken. Die Form des Grundstücks gab den Ausschlag dafür, bei dem Gebäude die Horizontale stärker zu betonen als die Vertikale. Auf eine Vorhangfassade in Dubai-typischer Ausprägung wurde zugunsten einer sich anpassenden Gebäudehülle verzichtet, die besser auf die aride Wüstenumgebung abgestimmt ist. Der abgerundete Grundriss des Gebäudes kombiniert die Effizienz übereinander geschichteter Geschosse mit reichhaltigen skulpturalen Möglichkeiten. Die neuartigen Geschosse lassen individuellere, kleine bis mittelgroße Bürokonfigurationen zu. Der Entwurf konzipiert die Gebäudehülle neu: Eine vom Boden bis zur Decke reichende Fensterwand mit perforierten Aluminiumblenden ist nicht nur ästhetisch gelungen, sondern sorgt auch für einen ökologischen, sinnvollen Sonnenschutz. Die Aluminiumhaut schirmt den Turm gegen das grelle Sonnenlicht und die Hitze ab, gewährt aber den Blick von drinnen nach draußen. Vor allem von den durch die vielen Kanten des Gebäudes zahlreich entstehenden Eckbüros wird dieser Blick großartig sein. Die abgerundeten Formen führen zu vielfältigen Variationsmöglichkeiten der äußeren Schicht. Während die Bauelemente dem Standard entsprechen, sind die Öffnungen alle unterschiedlich.

RMJM

Capital Gate Tower / Abu Dhabi

~ RMJM is a global architectural studio with offices across Europe, the Middle East and Africa, Asia-Pacific and the Americas. The firm's output encompasses architecture, sustainable design, urbanism, masterplanning, interior design, research and development. The combination of international expertise with an in-depth knowledge of regional markets allows RMJM to solve the most complex architectural challenges to offer dynamic solutions that are sympathetic to local culture and traditions.

~ RMJM ist ein weltweit engagiertes Architekturbüro mit Niederlassungen in Europa, dem Mittleren Osten und Afrika, in der Asien-Pazifik-Region sowie in Nord- und Südamerika. Die Mitarbeiter beschäftigen sich mit Architektur, nachhaltiger Gestaltung, Stadtplanung, Innenarchitektur, Forschung und Entwicklung. Durch die Verbindung von internationalem Fachwissen und profunden Kenntnissen regionaler Märkte kann RMJM auch hochkomplexe architektonische Herausforderungen meistern und dynamische Lösungen anbieten, die sich in die örtliche Kultur und ihre Traditionen einfügen.

~ CAPITAL GATE TOWER

Client: ADNEC (Abu Dhabi National Exhibitions Company)

Height: 160 m

Storeys: 35 (18 for hotel, 15 for offices, 2 for plant rooms)

Total Built-up Area: 53,100 m²

Total Office Area: 20,900 m²

Total Hotel Area: 25,050 m²

Inclination: 18 degrees

Under construction (start 2007)

Certified by the Guinness World Records as "the World's Furthest Leaning Man-made Tower", RMJM conceived Capital Gate Tower as the centre-piece for Abu Dhabi's first freehold development – comprising hotels, commercial buildings, residential and serviced apartment complexes and mixed-use developments. Capital Gate was the first tower to be built and therefore destined to be a landmark building to anchor the site. Distinguished by a striking organic form, featuring a cantilevered tea lounge and open-air pool deck, the building provides a unique presence on the city skyline and a memorable identity to the exhibition centre. A sculptural stainless steel 'splash' flows down the front to form the hotel entrance canopy, while also acting as a solar shading device for the building and grandstand seating. Structurally, this challenging building sits on an intensive distribution of 490 piles which have been drilled 30 m underground to accommodate the gravitational, wind and seismic forces caused by the distinctive lean of the building. A free-form internal atrium with a glass roof brings natural light and space deep into the tower, while external lighting is designed to minimise light pollution and energy consumption, with low-level landscape lighting and compact LED clusters integrated into the façade steel glazing system.

Capital Gate Tower, der laut Guinness-Buch der Rekorde „am stärksten geneigte Turm der Erde" wurde von RMJM als Herzstück von Abu Dhabis wichtigstem Flächenentwicklungsprojekt entworfen; zu dem Projekt gehören Hotels, Gewerbeimmobilien, Wohnhäuser und Apartments mit Service sowie Gebäude mit gemischter Nutzung. Seine markante organische Form macht den Turm zu etwas Besonderem, ebenso wie der auskragende Teesaal und das Schwimmbecken unter freiem Himmel. Capital Gate drückt der Skyline von Abu Dhabi seinen einzigartigen Stempel auf und ist ein erstklassiges Aushängeschild für das Messegelände. Eine „Welle" aus Edelstahl fließt an der Seite herunter und bildet den gigantischen Baldachin für den Hoteleingang. Gleichzeitig fungiert sie als Sonnenschutz für das Gebäude und die Tribüne des angrenzenden Stadions. Getragen wird die anspruchsvolle Konstruktion von 490 Pfeilern, die 30 Meter tief in der Erde verankert wurden. Sie sollen die Eigenlast, die Windlast sowie eventuell auftretende seismische Kräfte aufnehmen – allesamt Kräfte, die durch die starke Neigung des Gebäudes verstärkt werden. Ein mit einem Glasdach versehenes Atrium bringt viel natürliches Licht in das Innere des Turms und sorgt für ein großzügiges Raumgefühl. Gleichzeitig wurde darauf geachtet, Lichtverschmutzung und Energieverbrauch durch sparsame Außenleuchten und in die Verglasung integrierte LED-Technik zu minimieren.

173

SCHWEGER ASSOCIATED ARCHITECTS

Dubai Pearl / Dubai

~ In 1964 Heinz Graaf and Peter Schweger founded the Graaf-Schweger partnership, renamed Schweger Associated Architects in 2009. With offices in different German cities and in Dubai, the firm's architecture consistently aims for holistic and seminal solutions, while focusing on quality and innovation, developing many energy-and resource-saving buildings. The office has implemented ambitious designs for prominent private, institutional and public clients, both in Germany and abroad. Projects range from cultural, residential, commercial and public buildings to the redevelopment of historic structures and masterplanning. With a series of projects currently under construction or at planning stage, Schweger Associated Architects successfully participates in national and international competitions.

~ Heinz Graaf und Peter Schweger gründeten 1964 das Büro Graaf-Schweger, das seit 2009 unter dem Namen Schweger Associated Architects firmiert und Büroniederlassungen in verschiedenen deutschen Städten und Dubai hat. Ihre Planungen zielen stets auf ganzheitliche und zukunftsorientierte Lösungen, geprägt ebenso von Qualität und Innovation wie von energie- und ressourcensparenden Gesamtkonzepten. Das Büro hat für namhafte private und öffentliche Auftraggeber und Institutionen anspruchsvolle Bauwerke im In- und Ausland geplant. Die Realisierungen umfassen Kulturbauten, Wohn- und Geschäftshäuser, öffentliche Gebäude sowie städtebauliche Maßnahmen zur Neugestaltung historischer Strukturen. Mit Erfolg nehmen die Architekten seit vielen Jahren an nationalen und internationalen Wettbewerben teil.

~ DUBAI PEARL

Client: Dubai Pearl

Total Built-up Area: 6,096 m² (including parking)

Parking: 15,500 parking spaces in a 5-level podium

Retail GLA: 176,784 m²

Total open space: 56% of the podium area

Landscaping: 35% of the project area

No. of entrances: 5

Population: 9,000 residents / 12,000 employees

Estimated completion: 2013 (start 2008)

Situated in the heart of "new Dubai", overlooking the Palm Jumeirah island, Dubai Pearl epitomises Dubai's new approach – with a dynamic and environmentally sustainable composition of high-rise buildings, transformed into a new building form that symbolises diversity, unity and efficiency. To enhance the relationship of Dubai Pearl with its surroundings, the building form changes at every observable angle – creating a charismatic and welcoming setting. An integrated urban community, Dubai Pearl is anchored by a dramatic tower – a new beacon on Dubai's skyline that celebrates design simplicity and the efficient use of space. Column-free rectangular floors allow complete flexibility of use and reveal unobstructed vistas at street level. The podium is the technical heart of the entire development, ensuring its functional capability. The architecture of the neighbouring buildings intercommunicates with the high-rises, and the low-rise city centre harmoniously interacts with the landscape, creating a unique character and sense of place.

Im Herzen des „neuen Dubai" mit Blick auf die Insel Palm Jumeirah verkörpert Dubai Pearl einen neuen Ansatz der Stadtplanung: mit dynamischen und ökologisch nachhaltigen Hochhäusern, die als Ensemble Vielfalt, Einheit und Effizienz symbolisieren. Damit sich Dubai Pearl harmonischer in sein Umfeld einfügt, ändert sich seine Form mit jedem neuen Blickwinkel, wodurch ein charismatisches und einladendes Ganzes entsteht. Dubai Pearl kann als ein in sich geschlossenes Quartier gesehen werden, das sich um einen expressiven Turm herum gruppiert – einem neuen Leuchtturm in der Skyline von Dubai, der für klares Design und effizienten Umgang mit dem Raum steht. Stützenfreie rechtwinklige Geschossdecken sorgen für völlige Flexibilität bei der Nutzung und gewähren eine ungehinderte Sicht auf die Straße. Das Podium bildet das technische Herz des Ensembles und stellt zahlreiche Funktionen zur Verfügung. Die Architektur der Nachbarbebauung steht im Dialog mit den Hochhäusern, während die niedrigeren Gebäude harmonisch mit der Landschaft interagieren. Das verleiht dem Ort einen besonderen Charakter und führt zu einer einzigartigen Raumwahrnehmung.

SOM

Burj Khalifa / Dubai with Adrian Smith FAIA, RIBA
Infinity Tower / Dubai
Rolex Tower / Dubai

~ Skidmore, Owings & Merrill (SOM) is one of the world's leading architecture, interior design, engineering and urban-planning firms, with a 75-year reputation for design excellence and a portfolio that includes some of the most important architectural accomplishments of the 20th and 21st centuries. Since its inception, SOM has been a leader in the research and development of specialised technologies, new processes and innovative ideas, many of which have had a palpable and lasting impact on the design profession and the physical environment. Maintaining offices in the US, UK, UAE and Asia, the firm's longstanding leadership in design and building technology has been honoured with more than 1,400 awards for quality, innovation and management.

~ Skidmore, Owings & Merrill (SOM) ist eines der weltweit wichtigsten Büros in den Bereichen Architektur, Innenarchitektur, Hochbau und Stadtplanung und steht seit 75 Jahren für exzellente Gestaltung. Zu seinem Portfolio gehören einige der wichtigsten Errungenschaften der Architektur des 20. und 21. Jahrhunderts. Seit seiner Gründung ist SOM führend in der Forschung und Entwicklung von Spezialverfahren, und viele seiner innovativen Ideen hatten nachhaltigen Einfluss sowohl auf die Design-Berufe als auch für die reale Umwelt. SOM hat Büros in den USA, in Großbritannien, den Vereinigten Arabischen Emiraten und in weiteren asiatischen Ländern. Seine langjährige Führerschaft in Sachen Planen und Bauen wurde bereits mit über 1.400 Auszeichnungen für Qualität, Innovation und Management gewürdigt.

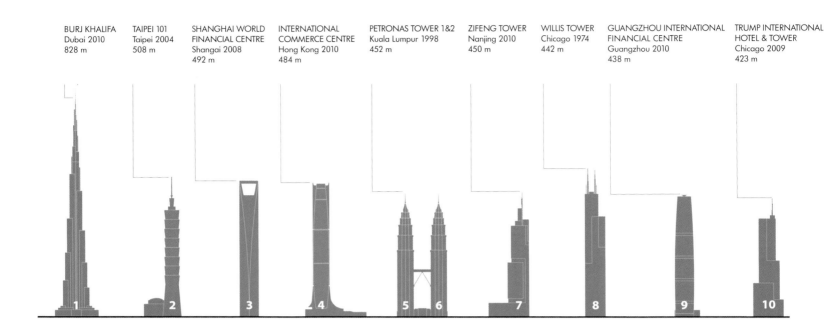

BURJ KHALIFA
Dubai 2010
828 m

TAIPEI 101
Taipei 2004
508 m

SHANGHAI WORLD
FINANCIAL CENTRE
Shangai 2008
492 m

INTERNATIONAL
COMMERCE CENTRE
Hong Kong 2010
484 m

PETRONAS TOWER 1&2
Kuala Lumpur 1998
452 m

ZIFENG TOWER
Nanjing 2010
450 m

WILLIS TOWER
Chicago 1974
442 m

GUANGZHOU INTERNATIONAL
FINANCIAL CENTRE
Guangzhou 2010
438 m

TRUMP INTERNATIONAL
HOTEL & TOWER
Chicago 2009
423 m

TALLEST OF THE TALL

Burj Khalifa is ranked number one in all three criteria for tall buildings of the Council on Tall Buildings and Urban Habitat (CTBUH). The CTBUH ranks the world's tallest buildings based on "Height to Architectural Top", "Height to Highest Occupied Floor" and "Height to Tip".

HEIGHT TO ARCHITECTURAL TOP

Burj Khalifa – 828 m
Taipei 101, Taiwan – 508 m
Shanghai World Financial Centre, China – 492 m
Petronas Towers, Malaysia – 452 m

HEIGHT TO HIGHEST OCCUPIED FLOOR

Burj Khalifa – 535 m
Shanghai World Financial Centre, China – 474 m
Taipei 101, Taiwan – 438 m
Willis Tower, Chicago – 413 m

HEIGHT TO TIP

Burj Khalifa – 828 m
Willis Tower, Chicago – 527 m
Taipei 101, Taiwan – 508 m
Shanghai World Financial Centre, China – 494 m

BURJ KHALIFA HOLDS THE FOLLOWING WORLD RECORDS

Tallest building in the world – surpassing Taipei 101 in Taiwan
Tallest man-made structure in the world – surpassing the KVLY-TV mast in North Dakota, USA
Tallest free-standing structure in the world – breaking the 31-year-old record of CN Tower in Toronto, Canada
Largest number of storeys in the world – 200, with 160 habitable storeys
Highest occupied floor in the world – Level 160
Highest outdoor observation deck in the world – Level 124
World record for vertical concrete pumping – 605 m
Tallest service elevator in the world – 504 m
Highest installation of an aluminium and glass façade

FACTS AT A GLANCE

Developer: Emaar Properties PJSC
Site Area: 104,210 m²
Project Area: 454,249 m²
Height: 828 m
Storeys: 200 with 160 habitable storeys
Built-up Area: 0.52 million m²
Weight of empty building: 500,000 t
Curtain wall area: 132,190 m³
Total reinforced steel used: 39,000 t
Total glass used for façade: 103,000 m²
Total stainless steel used for cladding: 15,500 m²
Completion: 2010 (start: 2004)

TOWER'S SPIRE VISIBLE FROM

60 MILES AWAY

PROJECT COST ABOUT

US $1.5 bn

330,000 m³
OF CONCRETE USED
IN CONSTRUCTION

22 MILLION
MAN-HOURS SPENT
BUILDING STRUCTURE

24,348
CLADDING PANELS

57 ELEVATORS
(9 M/SEC)

3,000 STAIRS

ON FLOOR 76
THE WORLD'S HIGHEST SWIMMING POOL

~ Burj Khalifa (formerly Burj Dubai) is positioned at the centre of Dubai's prestigious "Downtown" development, and is the tallest building in the world (surpassing Taipei 101 in Taiwan). It also holds the record for being the tallest man-made structure in the world (surpassing the KVLY-TV mast in the US) and the tallest free-standing structure in the world (breaking the 31-year record of the CN Tower in Canada). Other mind-boggling statistics include: the largest number of storeys in the world (200 – with 160 habitable); the highest occupied floor in the world (level 160); the highest outdoor observation deck in the world (level 124); the world record for vertical concrete pumping (605 m); the tallest service elevator in the world (504 m); and the world record for the highest installation of an aluminium and glass façade. The goal of the Burj Khalifa was not simply to be the world's highest building – rather, it was to embody the world's highest aspirations. The design combines cultural influences with cutting-edge technology to achieve a high-performance building. The multi-use tower features an Armani Hotel, private residences, offices and retail. The structural system can be described as a "buttressed" core: each wing, with its own high-performance concrete core and perimeter columns, buttressing the others via a hexagonal central core. The result is a tower that is extremely stiff torsionally. The advantage of the structure's stepping and shaping is to "confuse" the wind consequently, wind vortexes never form because the wind encounters a different building shape at every tier. SOM applied a rigorous geometry to the tower that aligns the central core and column elements to form the structure. Each tier of the building steps back in a spiral stepping pattern up the building, decreasing the tower's mass as it rises towards the sky.

~ Der Burj Khalifa (früher Burj Dubai) steht im Zentrum des prestigeträchtigen Stadtentwicklungsgebiets von Downtown Dubai. Er ist das höchste Gebäude der Welt (höher als der Taipei 101 in Taiwan). Er ist außerdem das höchste Bauwerk der Welt (höher als der KVLY-Mast in den USA) und das höchste freistehende Bauwerk der Erde (womit der 31 Jahre alte Rekord des CN Tower in Kanada gebrochen wurde). Zu weiteren schwindelerregenden Fakten gehören: die meisten Stockwerke der Welt (200, von denen 160 bewohnbar sind), die höchste genutzte Etage der Welt (die 160.), die höchste Aussichtsplattform (Ebene 124), der Weltrekord im vertikalen Betonpumpen (605 m), der höchste Technik-Fahrstuhl der Welt (504 m) sowie die höchste Aluminium-und-Glas-Fassade der Welt. Mit dem Burj Khalifa sollte nicht das höchste Gebäude der Welt errichtet, sondern auch den höchsten Ansprüchen eine konkrete Form gegeben werden. Die Gestaltung verbindet vielfältige kulturelle Einflüsse mit modernster Technik und lässt so ein Hochleistungsgebäude entstehen. In dem Mehrzweckturm befinden sich ein Armani-Hotel, Privatwohnungen, Büros und Einzelhandelsgeschäfte. Das Gebäude besteht aus drei Hauptsäulen, die sich gegenseitig abstützen: Jeder Flügel stützt mit seinem eigenen stabilen Betonkern und seinen äußeren Pfeilern die anderen Flügel ab. In der Turmmitte macht eine sechseckige Achse den Burj Khalifa extrem verwindungssteif. Die unterschiedlichen Abstufungen des Komplexes haben unter anderem die Funktion, den Wind zu „verwirren". Auf diese Weise können keine extremen Verwirbelungen entstehen, denn auf jeder Ebene trifft der Wind auf anders geformte Elemente. Wie eine große Wendeltreppe windet sich der Burj Khalifa nach oben, wobei er auf seinem Weg in den Himmel immer schlanker wird.

~ ARMANI HOTEL DUBAI

The Armani Hotel in Dubai is the first hotel designed and developed by the international fashion designer, Giorgio Armani. Reflecting the elegance, simplicity and sophisticated comfort that define Armani's signature style, the hotel is the realisation of the designer's long-held dream to bring his sophisticated style to life in a three-dimensional capacity. Every detail bears the Armani signature – from the Eramosa stone floors and zebra wood panels to the bespoke furnishings and personally designed hotel amenities. Sophisticated colours, clean lines and unique textures blend together seamlessly with the tower's streamlined architecture to create an atmosphere of serenity where guests can retreat into a world of minimalist elegance. With its own dedicated tower entrance, the hotel features 160 luxuriously appointed guest rooms, occupying the concourse level to Level 8 and Levels 38 and 39 of the Burj Khalifa. The hotel has eight restaurants, an exclusive Armani/Privé night club, an Armani/Ballroom, a 30,000 m² conference and banquet facility and the multi-functional outdoor Armani/Pavilion. Also first to the region are the three retail outlets: Armani/Dolci, Armani/Fiori and Armani/Galleria.

Mit dem Armani-Hotel in Dubai hat der berühmte Modedesigner Giorgio Armani zum ersten Mal ein Hotel konzipiert. Typisch für Armani sind Eleganz, Schlichtheit und gehobener Komfort, Charakteristika, die sich auch in seinem Hotel widerspiegeln. Der Designer hat seinen sehr alten Traum in die dreidimensionale Realität umgesetzt. Jedes Detail trägt die Handschrift von Armani: von den Marmorböden und Wandvertäfelungen aus Zebranoholz bis zur maßgeschneiderten Einrichtung. Die Farbpalette, die klaren Linien und die einzigartigen Stoffe werden eins mit der avantgardistischen Architektur des Turms. Zusammen erschaffen sie eine Atmosphäre der Ruhe und Klarheit. Hotelgäste können sich in eine Welt der minimalistischen Eleganz zurückziehen. Das Hotel hat einen eigenen Eingang, es verfügt über 160 luxuriöse Zimmer, die sich von der Versammlungsebene bis zum achten Stock sowie über die Ebenen 38 und 39 des Burj Khalifa erstrecken. Das Hotel wartet auf mit acht Restaurants, einem exklusiven Nachtclub, einem Festsaal, 30.000 m² für Konferenzen und Bankette sowie mit einem Mehrzweck-Pavillon im Freien. Außerdem bietet das Armani-Hotel drei Verkaufsläden: Armani Dolci, Armani Fiori und Armani Galleria.

~ INFINITY TOWER
Site Area: 3,026.50 m^2
Project Area: 365,760 m^2
Height: 307 m
Storeys: 73
Under construction

Designed to stand out in a city of extraordinary architecture, once completed, the Infinity Tower will be the tallest twisting tower in the world. Situated in Dubai Marina, it will have over 450 residential units, ranging from studios to full-floor penthouses, and other amenities including an outdoor pool, health spa, gymnasium, lounges, conference centres, crèche, retail outlets and an arcade. The building's unique metal-clad helix form is its most striking feature and a direct expression of its structural framework. The column superstructure rotates 90 degrees – one degree at each floor – forming the tower's unique helix shape around a core of reinforced concrete and an exterior of corrosion-resistant titanium. The structure is clad in prefabricated unitised metal panels which are repetitive and identical on each floor, allowing for rapid and precise construction and providing insulation and protection from the highly corrosive gulf environment. To protect against Dubai's hot desert climate, vision glass is recessed between the columns, providing solar shading and balconies for each apartment. Additional shading in the form of perforated metal screens minimises the glass tint required and creates dynamic shadow patterns within. Infinity Tower has already been singled out as a regional landmark that will become synonymous with Dubai's waterfront.

In einer Stadt mit außergewöhnlicher Architektur soll sich der Infinity Tower aus dem Umfeld herausheben. Vollendet wird er der höchste verdrehte Turm der Welt sein. Im Stadtviertel Dubai Marina wird er mit über 450 Wohneinheiten aufwarten – von Einzimmerapartments bis zu sehr geräumigen Penthouses. Dazu kommen Annehmlichkeiten wie ein Swimmingpool im Freien, ein Wellnessbereich, Sportmöglichkeiten, Gesellschafts- und Konferenzräume, ein Kinderhort, Geschäfte und eine Spielhalle. Die einzigartige metallverkleidete Helix ist das auffälligste Gebäudemerkmal. Der säulenartige Bau ist um 90 Grad verdreht (ein Grad pro Stockwerk), wodurch die Helixform entsteht, die sich um einen Kern aus verstärktem Beton windet. Die Außenhülle besteht aus wetterfestem Titan. Vor die Fassade werden vorgefertigte Metallpaneele gehängt; sie sind in jedem Stockwerk gleich. Das ermöglicht eine schnelle und präzise Bauweise, sorgt für gute Dämmung und schützt gegen das sehr korrosive Golfklima. Als Schutz gegen die Wüstenhitze werden getönte Scheiben zurückgesetzt zwischen den Stützen eingelassen, so dass weniger direktes Licht auf die Balkone und in die Wohnungen gelangt. Perforierte Metallschirme sorgen für zusätzlichen Sonnenschutz und so müssen die Scheiben nicht so stark abgetönt werden. Schon jetzt zeigt sich, dass der Infinity Tower ein Wahrzeichen der Region und der Uferpromenade werden wird.

~ ROLEX TOWER
Site Area: 2,731 m²
Project Area: 198,120 m²
Height: 235 m
Storeys: 59
Completion: 2010

Rolex Tower is situated on Dubai's main artery, the Sheikh Zayed Road. Like a fine timepiece, the tower's design is classic and elegant, with a quiet neighbourhood presence amongst the dynamism of Sheikh Zayed Road's skyscrapers and multi-lane traffic. The building is veiled in a high-performance curtain wall of fritted green glass which fades as it ascends, expressing the height of the tower while providing shade from the sun, crucial in Dubai's arid climate. Both commercial and residential programmes are incorporated into the tower, with 30 floors of office space, 25 floors of apartments, and two residential penthouses on the uppermost floors. Certain parts of the interiors were also designed by SOM, including the ground-floor lobbies. A sculptural installation, "Soundwave" by lighting artist James Clar, is an interpretation of the artist's voice saying "Rolex Tower", adding a sense of intrigue to the building's entrance. Rolex Tower demonstrates a commitment to high-quality design standards for city planning, clarifying an urban vision by fitting seamlessly into Dubai's existing cityscape through classic, clean design, while providing residents with a desirable place to live. Through tasteful luxury and quiet minimalism, Rolex Tower sets a new standard for high-end development in the Middle East and beyond.

Der Rolex Tower steht an der Hauptverkehrsader von Dubai, der Sheikh Zayed Road. Wie bei einer kostbaren Uhr ist auch hier das Design klassisch und elegant. Gleichsam als ein ruhiger Nachbar fügt sich der Turm in die Dynamik der Wolkenkratzer und des Verkehrs ein. Die Fassade besteht aus einer leistungsstarken Verkleidung aus grünem Fritteglas, das nach oben immer heller wird. Dies unterstreicht die Höhe des Turms und ist gleichzeitig ein effektiver Sonnenschutz – im ariden Klima von Dubai äußerst wichtig. Das Bauwerk ist sowohl für gewerbliche Zwecke als auch für Wohnnutzung ausgelegt: 30 Stockwerke Büroraum und 25 Stockwerke mit Wohnungen stehen zur Verfügung. In den obersten Etagen befinden sich zwei Penthouses. SOM hat außerdem einige Elemente der Innenausstattung entworfen, darunter die Foyers im Erdgeschoss. Dort wertet die Installation „Soundwave" von James Clar den Eingang auf. Mithilfe eines Computerprogramms hat der Lichtkünstler die von ihm selbst gesprochenen Worte „Rolex Tower" in eine skulpturale Form transformiert. Der Rolex Tower ist ein Bekenntnis zu hochwertigen Standards in der Stadtplanung. Er setzt eine urbane Vision um, indem er sich nahtlos in die existierende Stadtlandschaft von Dubai einfügt. Dies geschieht mittels einer klassischen, klaren Gestaltung, die den Ort für seine Bewohner sehr attraktiv macht. Mit seinem geschmackvollen Luxus und ruhigen Minimalismus setzt der Rolex Tower einen neuen Standard für das Luxussegment im Nahen Osten und darüber hinaus.

SMAQ

Xeritown / Dubai

with X-Architects

~ Founded by Sabine Müller and Andreas Quednau, SMAQ is a Berlin-based collaborative studio for architecture, urbanism and research that focuses on urban design and architecture as a (re)active practice of "making something which cannot perform without the assistance of its environment". SMAQ's work has been widely published and exhibited, most recently at the International Architecture Biennials in Rotterdam and Venice.

~ SMAQ, gegründet von Sabine Müller und Andreas Quednau, ist ein Berliner Büro für Architektur, Stadtplanung und Stadtforschung, dessen Fokus auf Stadtgestaltung und Architektur liegt, verstanden als ein „Schaffens von etwas, das sich nicht ohne die Hilfe der kontextuellen Bedingungen darstellen kann". Die Arbeiten von SMAQ wurden vielfach veröffentlicht und ausgestellt, so auch auf den internationalen Architekturbiennalen in Rotterdam und Venedig.

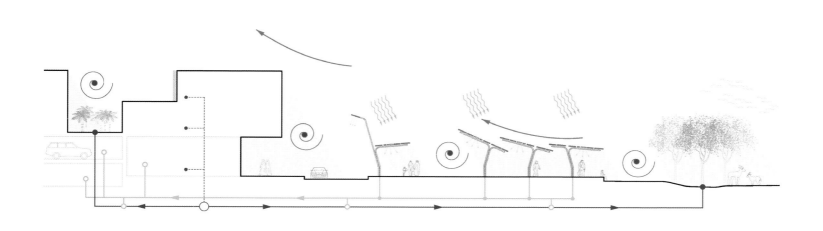

~ XERITOWN
Lighting Design: Reflexion – Infrastructure: Buro Happold
Client: Dubai Properties
Site Area: 590,000 m²
Building Area: 214,000 m² – Gross Floor Area: 486,000 m²
Building Coverage Ratio: 26% – Gross Floor Ratio: 83%
Storeys: 12 above ground
Max. Height: 45 m
Landscape Area: 265,450 m²
Ongoing

Xeritown is a sustainable mixed-use development in Dubailand, an outer suburb of Dubai, which takes the desert and local climate as a context within which the urban form emerges, working with the natural environment rather than against it. The built-up area has been compressed to occupy just 50% of the site. As an immediate reaction to the conditions of the sun and to achieve a compact shaded fabric, the structure is defined by alternating narrow pedestrian alleys and small squares which are typical of traditional Arabic towns. This urban tissue is divided into elongated islands that are orientated to gain from the prevailing winds crossing the site. Natural ventilation is enhanced by a rugged skyline breaking up air flows on the scale of both low-rises and towers. A focal part of the design lies between the landscape and the urban fabric. A shading device composed of photovoltaic panels provides valuable energy to the site. Solutions that focus on resource-saving principles and creating a pleasant environment for social interaction have determined the design of the architectural typologies, all of which benefit climatically and visually from the proximity to the landscape. The project applies a multitude of strategies for achieving an ecological quality, such as reducing energy demand by minimising solar gains thanks to northeast orientation, natural ventilation and earth pipes, dimmable LED street lighting, photovoltaic panels to generate low-voltage direct current electricity and rooftop turbines; strategies for the conversion of resources by reducing the demand for potable water thanks to low water-use appliances, grey water recycling and water saving for irrigation systems, low-maintenance landscaping, the re-use of soil on site and waste-recycling facilities, and strategies for reducing carbon emissions with easy-access public transport and extensively shaded, well-ventilated pedestrian and cycling routes. The project won the Regional Acknowledgement Prize of the Holcim Award 2008 for Sustainable Construction.

Xeritown ist ein nachhaltiges Stadterweiterungsprojekt mit gemischter Nutzung in Dubailand, einem Außenbezirk von Dubai in der Wüste. Ausgangspunkt für den Entwurf ist das lokale Klima; die urbane Form entwickelte sich aus den natürlichen Gegebenheiten. Als Reaktion auf die starke Sonneneinstrahlung wurde die Bebauung auf 50 % der Grundstücksfläche komprimiert, mit dem Resultat einer engen, sich selbst verschattenden städtischen Struktur. Enge Fußgängerstraßen und kleine Plätze prägen das Gefüge und erinnern an traditionelle Bauweisen. Das Raster der Stadt ist in streifenartige Inseln zerlegt und so ausgerichtet, dass es von den vorherrschenden Windrichtungen profitiert. Eine unregelmäßige, den Luftstrom brechende Skyline aus niedrigen Gebäuden und Türmen unterstützt die natürliche Belüftung. Eine der herausragenden Leistungen des Entwurfs ist das ausgewogene Verhältnis zwischen Bebauung und Landschaft. Ressourcensparende Prinzipien und eine dem Klima angemessene Umgebung für soziale Interaktionen haben bestimmte Bautypologien – wie Apartmentgebäude, Townhouses, Hotels und kulturelle Einrichtungen – hervorgebracht, die sowohl klimatisch als auch visuell von der Nähe zur Landschaft profitieren. Das gesamtstädtische Energiekonzept sieht hochentwickelte Technologien zur Solar- und Windenergiegewinnung sowie zur Energieeinsparung vor, beispielsweise durch die Nord-Süd-Ausrichtung der Gebäude, die eine starke Sonnenerwärmung verhindern soll, durch natürliche Belüftung und Erdregister sowie mittels einer bedarfsorientierten LED-Straßenbeleuchtung. Der Trinkwasserverbrauch soll durch effiziente Haushaltsgeräte und die Aufbereitung von Grauwasser für die Bewässerung gering gehalten werden. Eine pflegeleichte Begrünung, Müll-Recycling und ein durch die Förderung des Fahrradfahrens und des öffentlichen Verkehrs möglichst geringer CO_2-Ausstoß sind weitere Maßnahmen. Das Projekt wurde mit dem Holcim Award 2008 für Nachhaltiges Bauen ausgezeichnet.

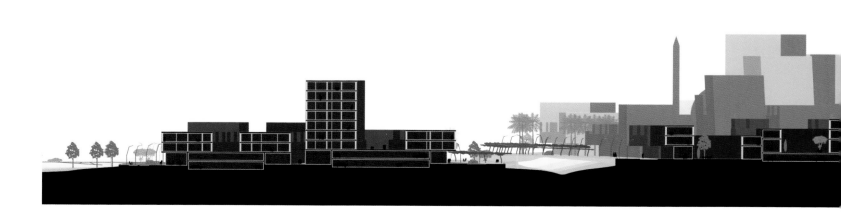

ADRIAN SMITH + GORDON GILL ARCHITECTURE

Meraas Tower / Dubai
1 Dubai / Dubai
Za'abeel Energy City / Dubai
Park Gate / Dubai

~ Adrian Smith + Gordon Gill Architecture is a partnership formed in 2006 by Adrian Smith, Gordon Gill and Robert Forest that is dedicated to the design of high-performance architecture in a wide range of typologies and scales – from low- and mid-rise residential, commercial and cultural buildings to mixed-use skyscrapers and new cities. The office uses a holistic, integrated design approach that explores symbiotic relationships with the natural environment and seeks to maximise energy efficiency and the potential for on-site energy generation from renewable sources. The practice is currently working on projects for clients in the UAE, Saudi Arabia, China, India, South Korea, Malaysia, Canada and the US. In early 2010, the partners created PositivEnergy Practice, an energy services, engineering and consulting company that conceives, designs, implements and manages energy performance, resource management and carbon reduction strategies for companies around the world.

~ Adrian Smith + Gordon Gill Architecture ist ein Zusammenschluss von Adrian Smith, Gordon Gill und Robert Forest. Seit 2006 entwerfen sie höchst energieeffiziente Gebäude für unterschiedliche Nutzungen in verschiedensten Größen – von niedrigen bis mittelhohen Wohngebäuden, Gewerbebauten und Kultureinrichtungen bis zu Wolkenkratzern für Mischnutzungen und neuen Städten. Das Büro arbeitet mit einem ganzheitlichen Entwurfsansatz, der symbiotische Beziehungen mit der umgebenden Natur einbezieht, nach einer höchstmöglichen Energieeffizienz strebt und das Potenzial einer Energieerzeugung vor Ort durch die Nutzung erneuerbarer Energien bestmöglich ausschöpft. Bearbeitet werden derzeit Projekte für Bauherren in den VAE, Saudi Arabien, China, Indien, Südkorea, Malaysia, Kanada und den USA. Anfang 2010 gründeten die Partner die Beratungsgesellschaft für Energieversorgung und Technik, PositivEnergy Practice, die weltweit Strategien für Energieeinsparung, Ressourcenmanagement und CO_2-Reduktion in Unternehmen entwickelt, ausgestaltet, umsetzt und betreut.

~ MERAAS TOWER
Client: Meraas Development
Height: 550 m
Floor Area: 600,000 m²
Storeys: 112
Ongoing

Meraas Tower combines simple geometric principles with new and emerging technologies to create a modern, soaring "tower of light" for Dubai. Like a prism, the tower has a series of faceted surfaces that increase the light and air travelling through the building. The faceted shapes maximise the energy derived from building-integrated photovoltaic panels. The facets also balance the natural light in the building's interior. The atrium spaces as the building ascends, allow for naturally ventilated sky gardens that activate the building form. Exposing the intermediate floors gives an illusion that the building is composed of four smaller towers stacked on top of one another. The tower has been designed to become a positive energy building with optimised orientation to maximise capturing all solar and wind energy. The open floors at various heights not only reduce the lateral wind load on structure, but also create opportunities to bring natural daylight into the building through the atrium. The project's landscaping offers both a relaxing and active environment.

Der Meraas Tower verbindet einfache geometrische Prinzipien mit neuer Technik und neuen Verfahren, um einen modernen, hoch aufragenden „Turm des Lichts" entstehen zu lassen. Ähnlich wie ein Prisma verfügt das Bauwerk über facettierte Oberflächen, die sehr viel Licht und Luft durch das Gebäude strömen lassen. Die Facettierung erhöht die Stromproduktion durch die integrierten Photovoltaikzellen. Die Facetten sorgen zudem für ein gleichmäßige Lichtverteilung im Gebäudeinneren. In den diversen Atrien entstehen natürlich belüftete Höhengärten, die die Form des Turms besonders zur Geltung bringen. Die Betonung der Zwischengeschosse befördert den Eindruck, dass das Gebäude aus vier kleineren Türmen besteht, die aufeinandergesetzt wurden. Der Turm ist für eine positive Energiebilanz konzipiert, durch seine Ausrichtung sollen Sonnen- und Windenergie bestmöglich ausgenutzt werden. Die Öffnungen auf verschiedenen Höhen verringern nicht nur die seitliche Windlast, sondern lassen auch mehr Tageslicht ins Innere dringen. Die mit dem Projekt einhergehende Gestaltung der Umgebung sorgt für ein gleichwohl entspannendes wie aktives Umfeld.

~ 1 DUBAI
Client: Meraas Development
Height: Shortest tower 600 m; tallest tower undisclosed
Floor Area: 1,784,257 m^2
Ongoing

A trio of "supertowers" of staggered heights, joined near the base, 1 Dubai will be one of the tallest and largest megastructures in the world. A city within a city, this giant mixed-use project will be the centrepiece of Dubai and its Jumeirah Gardens development. On its tripodal base, 1 Dubai rises over a canal that forms a central oasis. Viewers will be able to gaze up through the great atrium-like space between the towers. At night, a virtual "fourth tower" – a giant beam of light – will lance through the atrium. On special occasions the oasis will transform itself into an events and performance space, with a floating stage surrounded by barges doubling as seating banks. High above, a series of three-storey skybridges, or "plazas in the sky", connect the towers as they taper upwards. These will afford breathtaking city and sea views, while helping to stabilise the towers structurally and facilitate inter-floor circulation. The structure will house two world-class hotels, office and retail space and some of the world's highest condominiums. The tallest tower will feature one of the world's highest and most exclusive club-observation decks. This project takes full advantage of cutting-edge sustainability technologies, with special emphasis on photovoltaics to generate solar energy.

Ein Trio aus „Supertürmen" von schwindelerregender Höhe, die an ihrer Basis verbunden sind – das ist 1 Dubai. Das Gebäude wird eines der höchsten und eindrucksvollsten der Welt sein. Als Stadt in der Stadt ist das für gemischte Nutzung vorgesehene 1 Dubai dazu auserkoren, das Herzstück von Dubai und den Jumeirah Gardens zu werden. Mit seinen drei Beinen überbrückt der Komplex einen Kanal, der eine zentrale Oase bildet. Passanten können durch die große atriumartige Öffnung zwischen den drei Türmen nach oben blicken. Nachts scheint ein virtueller „vierter Turm" – ein riesiger Lichtstrahl – durch das Atrium. Zu besonderen Anlässen wird sich die Oase in einen Veranstaltungsort verwandeln: Um eine schwimmende Bühne werden Lastkähne gruppiert, in denen die Zuschauer platziert werden können. Dazu kommt modernste Beschallungs- und Beleuchtungstechnik. Weiter oben finden sich voluminöse „Himmelsbrücken", die die sich nach oben verjüngenden Türme auf verschiedenen Höhen miteinander verbinden. Diese „Himmelsplätze" bieten einen atemberaubenden Blick auf die Stadt und das Meer, während sie gleichzeitig die Türme stabilisieren und auch für die Belüftung zwischen den Geschossen sorgen. Das Gebäude wird zwei Spitzenhotels beherbergen sowie Büroräume, Geschäfte und Wohnungen, die zu den höchsten der Welt zählen werden. Der höchste der drei Türme wartet mit einer der exklusivsten Aussichtsplattformen der Welt auf. Das Projekt nutzt modernste Verfahren für nachhaltiges Bauen, mit dem Schwerpunkt auf Energieerzeugung durch Photovoltaik.

~ ZA'ABEEL ENERGY CITY
Masterplan
Client: Meraas Development
Site Area: 92 hectares

The Energy Development masterplan has been positioned as a centre for commerce and residential development and will embody modern, sustainable living, work and play. With rail connections to Jumeirah Gardens and convenient proximity to the Burj Khalifa and the downtown district, the project is set to be a vibrant mixed-use area of Dubai. The generative concept behind the Masterplan is the development of memorable places that define sustainable districts and neighbourhoods and the creation of a major new civic park which can be accessed through shaded passageways for pedestrian and bicycle use along with multi-modal transport. The development has the potential to become a self-contained, mixed-use environment, achieving Dubai's first LEED platinum rating for community design. Office and hotel use will add interest along the main boulevard and throughout the development, effectively reinforcing this new business hub – with connected convention and hospitality functions nearby. Luxury residential lofts define the perimeter of the project, providing a distinctive and intimate living experience. In addition to creating memorable urban places, the concept draws on patterns in Islamic textiles, architectural ornamentation and traditional village design traditions, re-interpreted for modern materials and lifestyles, to create variation in landscapes, while adding texture and scale to the development.

Der Masterplan zur Energieentwicklung sieht ein Gewerbe- und Wohngebiet vor, das modernes, nachhaltiges Wohnen und Arbeiten ermöglichen soll. Bahnverbindungen zu Jumeirah Gardens, zum Burj Khalifa und ins Stadtzentrums sollen eine pulsierende Zone mit gemischter Nutzung entstehen lassen. Die Grundidee des Masterplans ist die Entwicklung von markanten Orten, von ganzen Vierteln, die für Nachhaltigkeit stehen, sowie die Errichtung eines großen Bürgerparks, den Fußgänger, Fahrradfahrer und andere Verkehrsteilnehmer auf schattigen Wegen erreichen können. Das Projekt hat das Potenzial, ein autarkes Gebiet zu werden und damit als erster Ort in Dubai eine LEED-Zertifizierung in Platin zu erhalten. Büros und Hotels werden dem Boulevard und der gesamten Entwicklungsfläche zusätzliche Attraktivität verleihen. Damit stärken sie die Stellung des Wirtschaftszentrums Dubai – auch mit ihren angeschlossenen Tagungs- und Bewirtungsmöglichkeiten. Luxus-Wohnlofts, die eine charakteristische und intime Wohnatmosphäre bieten, umschließen das Bauprojekt. Das Konzept greift auf Muster islamischer Stoffe zurück sowie auf islamische Bauornamentik und traditionelle Dorfgestaltung. Diese Elemente wurden neu interpretiert und auf moderne Materialien und Lebensweisen übertragen. Dadurch entsteht eine neue Stadtlandschaft, die dem Projekt gleichzeitig Struktur und Größe verleiht.

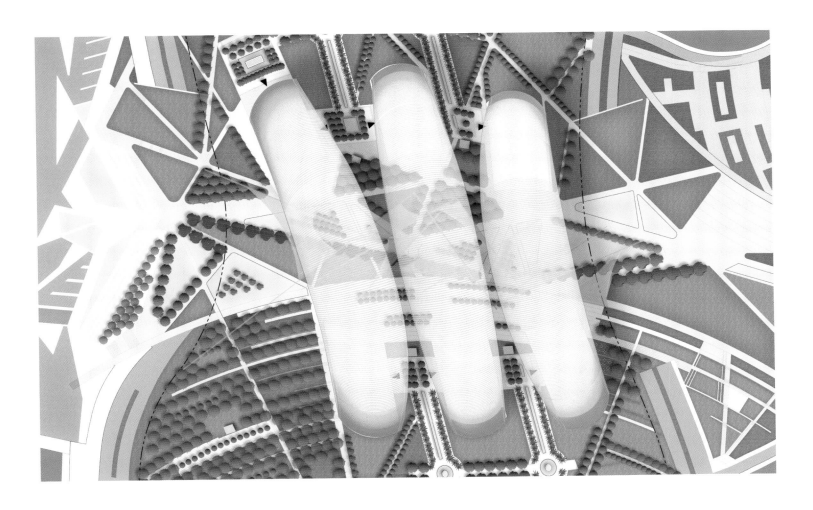

~ PARK GATE
Client: Meraas Development
Height: 111 m
Floor Area: 464,515 m²
Storeys: 34/37
Ongoing

Park Gate is a mixed-use development comprising office, hotel and retail that creates a visual portal in the surrounding park. Six gently curving towers, arranged in facing pairs, connect at the top by three vaulted canopies, surrounding a unique urban enclave inspired by the Middle East's traditional souks. This central plaza, further protected by micro-canopies, boasts expanses of drought-tolerant greenery and reflecting pools. From balconies and sky gardens in the surrounding towers, users will enjoy inspiring vistas of this outdoor "great hall", featuring indigenous, salt-water-tolerant plants and reflecting pools that also act as thermal sinks, absorbing heat during the day and releasing it at night. High above, the main canopies perform three sustainability functions in one: harvesting solar energy through photovoltaics on top; creating shade which reduces heat gain in the towers, reducing temperatures on the ground by 10 to 15 degrees; and incorporating trellises from which hanging plants can grow in a thriving microclimate irrigated by a grey water misting system. In the towers, whose sculpted form completes the curvature of the canopies, more sustainable design features and strategies are deployed. The towers are oriented to limit solar exposure and allow circulation of gulf breezes throughout the development. Landscaped sky gardens on some floors provide access to the outdoors and allow natural light to penetrate the interiors. The towers are oriented to slightly turn towards each other, heightening the sense of ensemble.

Park Gate ist ein Bauprojekt mit gemischter Nutzung für Büros, Hotels und Einzelhandel, das ein visuelles Tor zum angrenzenden Park sein soll. Sechs leicht gekrümmte Türme stehen sich paarweise gegenüber und sind an den Dächern durch gewölbte Hauben miteinander verbunden. Sie umschließen eine einzigartige städtische Enklave, die von den traditionellen Suks inspiriert ist. Der zentrale Platz, der von weiteren kleineren Überdachungen geschützt wird, ist großflächig mit trockenheitsverträglichen Pflanzen begrünt. Die Balkone und Höhengärten der umstehenden Türme gewähren den Nutzern anregende Einblicke in dieses „Palais" im Freien. Zu sehen gibt es heimische salzwasserbeständige Pflanzen und Reflexionsbecken, die für einen thermalen Ausgleich sorgen, indem sie tagsüber Wärme aufnehmen und nachts abgeben. Hoch oben kommen den Hauptüberdachungen wichtige Funktionen in Sachen Nachhaltigkeit zu: Sie produzieren Solarenergie mittels ihrer Photovoltaikzellen, sie spenden den Gebäuden unter ihnen Schatten, was die Temperaturen am Boden um 10–15 Grad reduziert, und sie verfügen über Rankgitter für Kletterpflanzen. Diese wachsen in einem fruchtbaren Mikroklima, das von einem Grauwasserverdunstungssystem gespeist wird. Auch in den Türmen steht Nachhaltigkeit im Vordergrund. Sie sind so ausgerichtet, dass sie der Sonne eine möglichst geringe Einfallfläche bieten und gleichzeitig die vom Golf kommenden Brisen gut in und zwischen den Gebäuden zirkulieren lassen. Begrünte Höhengärten auf einigen Etagen bieten Zugang ins Freie und lassen das Tageslicht ins Innere dringen. Die Türme sind leicht zueinander ausgerichtet, so dass der Eindruck eines Ensembles verstärkt wird.

STUDIED IMPACT

10MW Tower / Abu Dhabi

~ Studied Impact is a multidisciplinary design studio, founded by Elizabeth Monoian and Robert Ferry, which focuses on the environmental impact of design. Through various projects in architecture, public artworks, new media and graphic design, they call attention to issues of resource and energy conservation. In 2010, the architects founded The Land Art Generator Initiative – a biennial international design competition that brings together artists, architects, scientists, landscape architects and engineers with the goal of designing and constructing public art installations that combine aesthetics with clean energy generation. The art pieces capture energy from nature, cleanly converting it into electricity, transforming and transmitting the electrical power to the grid's connection point.

~ Studied Impact ist ein interdisziplinäres Designbüro, das von Elizabeth Monoian und Robert Ferry gegründet wurde und sich in erster Linie mit den ökologischen Aspekten einer Konstruktion beschäftigt. Mit den unterschiedlichsten Projekten in den Bereichen Architektur, Kunst im öffentlichen Raum, Neue Medien und Grafikdesign schaffen sie Aufmerksamkeit für die Themen Rohstoff- und Energieeinsparung. Aus ihren Entwürfen sollen nachhaltige Lebensräume für zukünftige Generationen hervorgehen. 2010 gründeten die Architekten die „Land Art Generator Initiative", einen zweijährlichen internationalen Gestaltungswettbewerb, der Künstler, Architekten, Wissenschaftler, Landschaftsplaner und Ingenieure zusammenbringt. Ihr Ziel ist es, öffentliche Kunstinstallationen zu kreieren, die Ästhetik mit sauberer Energieerzeugung in Einklang bringen. Die Kunstwerke nehmen Energie aus der Natur auf und konvertieren sie auf saubere Art und Weise in Strom, den sie dann in das Netz einspeisen.

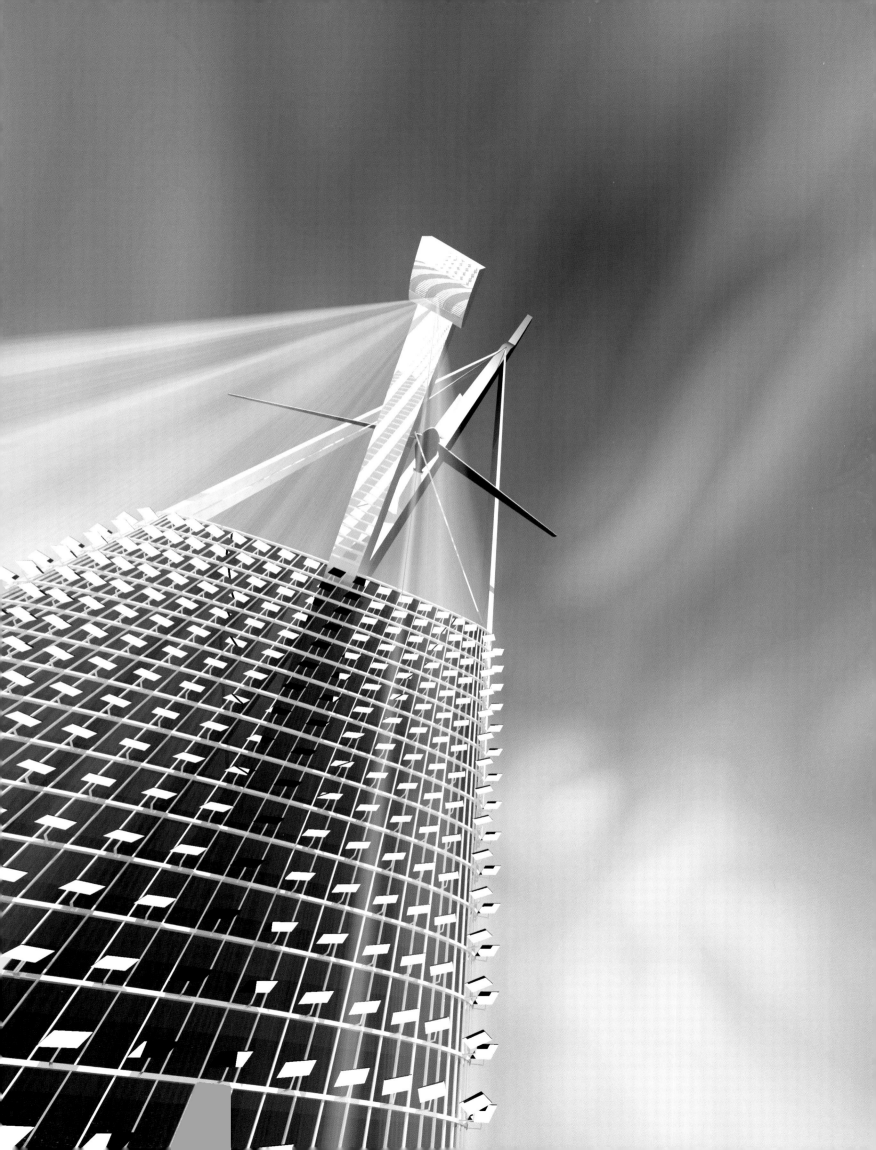

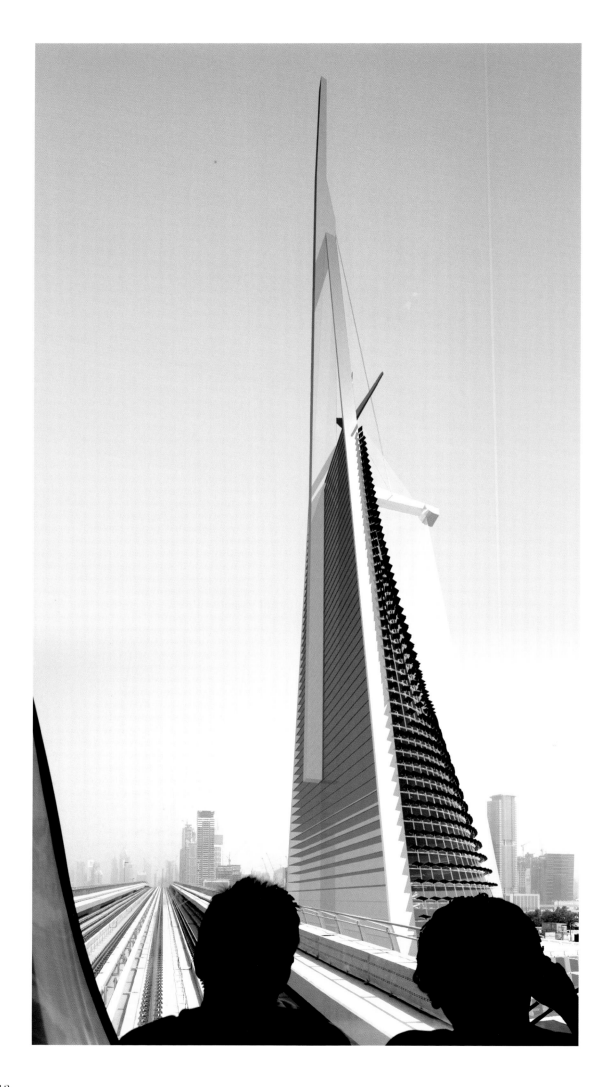

~ 10MW TOWER

The 10MW Tower is designed to be as much an aesthetic renewable energy power plant as an inhabited skyscraper. The building creates energy through three active systems: a horizontal axis wind turbine, a concentrated solar power armature and a solar updraught tower. By producing nearly nine times more energy than its own demand load, it can significantly contribute to the power load demand of the surrounding neighbourhood. The tower will neutralise its impact in less than 20 years through the clean energy it will generate. The shape of the tower's southern façade is derived from the geometry that provides the heliostatic mirrors. Inside the central collector, molten salt is heated by the mirrors to 500°C to produce steam for a generator. The mirrors serve as shading devices to the façade which is further protected from solar heat gain by a double curtain wall. This wall creates a greenhouse effect which continuously draughts upwards, passively cooling the building while actively running a wind turbine. The podium roof is a garden that provides a welcome haven for those working or living in the tower, with irrigation coming from the condensation of the building's air-handling units.

Der 10MW Tower ist die ästhetische Ausgestaltung eines Kraftwerks für erneuerbare Energien und gleichzeitig ein Wohnhochhaus. Das Gebäude erzeugt Energie mit Hilfe dreier Systeme: eine Horizontalachsen-Windturbine, eine starke Sonnenenergieanlage sowie ein Aufwindkraftwerk. Damit produziert der Turm neunmal so viel Energie wie er selbst benötigt und kann den Gebäuden in seiner Umgebung einen großen Teil abgeben. In weniger als 20 Jahren wird der Turm seine eigene Energiebilanz ausgeglichen haben. Das Aussehen der Südfassade ist den hier angebrachten Spezialspiegeln geschuldet. Sie leiten das Sonnenlicht auf den zentralen Absorber, in dessen Innern geschmolzenes Salz auf 500 Grad Celsius erhitzt wird. Mit dieser Hitze wird Dampf für einen Generator erzeugt. Die Spiegel spenden der Fassade gleichzeitig Schatten, zusätzlich wird sie durch eine doppelte vorgehängte Wand vor Überhitzung geschützt. Die Wand hat einen kühlenden Effekt, da an ihr immer warme Luft nach oben strömt und das dahinterliegende Gebäude kühlt. Gleichzeitig treibt der aufsteigende Luftstrom eine Windturbine an. Der Dachgarten ist ein Ort der Ruhe. Seine Bewässerung erfolgt mittels des ständig entstehenden Niederschlags aus der Lüftungsanlage.

X-ARCHITECTS

Mosque / Abu Dhabi
Museum of Religious Tolerance / Dubai
The White Hotel / Abu Dhabi

~ Founded in Dubai in 2003 by Ahmed Al-Ali and Farid Esmaeil, X-Architects operates a critical design approach which harnesses the inherent complexity in building and construction to produce schemes that are adaptable. Design and strategic decisions operate in tandem with the typical constraints and unforeseen developments of projects large or small – accepting change and adjustments in a productive and invigorating way is central to the progressive practice of X-Architects.

~ X-Architects wurde 2003 von Ahmed Al-Ali und Farid Esmaeil in Dubai gegründet. Mit einem kritischen Entwurfsansatz, der die Komplexität jedes Gebäudes und jeder Konstruktion nutzt, entwickeln sie anpassungsfähige Pläne. Die gestalterischen und strategischen Entscheidungen sind beeinflusst von den typischen Beschränkungen und unvorhersehbaren Entwicklungen bei großen und kleinen Projekten. So sind Veränderungen und Anpassungen als produktive und verstärkende Elemente ein zentraler Bestandteil der fortschrittlichen Arbeitsweise von X-Architects.

~ MOSQUE
Ongoing

Since the beginning of Islamic history, the mosque has had many different functions besides being a place for prayer. It is one of the most important "places" in the Muslim landscape where people go not only to pray but for social interaction and activities. A mosque should therefore be considered an urban element that is at the heart of its city and community; a main point of connection, where people can meet in a welcoming environment. The design strategy for this project is to enlarge the existing Sculpture Plaza to create an attractive public space as a physical and metaphorical connection between the Sculpture Park and the Pray Area. The journey between the two is a passage from public to semi-public to private. The Pray Area combines traditional elements in a modern interpretation. In the form of a square – the perfect shape as there is no hierarchy between the parts – so symbolising the core concept of Islam where everyone is equal in the eyes of Allah. The traditional dome is "sliced" in a unique geometrical weave of arcs to create an architectural module which will provide an intimate and peaceful space with natural light seeping through. This spiritual object will build a strong character in the urban environment and a powerful landmark within the community. To respect people's privacy, two wings will host separate services for men and women. The ablution and prayer areas are also separated from the rest of the complex by an arcade with a traditional Mashrabiya screen. A poetic garden with a water element to symbolise paradise closes off the outer area while providing a peaceful setting for the mosque. This design is a rich kaleidoscope of layers that makes a contemporary statement for a traditional building in the capital city of Abu Dhabi.

Seit jeher ist die Moschee ein Ort, den die Muslime nicht nur zum Beten, sondern auch für gesellschaftlichen Austausch und andere Aktivitäten nutzen. Eine Moschee sollte daher als urbanes Element betrachtet werden, das im Herzen der Stadt und der Gemeinschaft steht – ein wichtiger Treffpunkt für die Menschen, mit einem einladenden Umfeld. Zum Entwurf von X-Architects gehört daher auch Vergrößerung der vorhandenen Sculpture Plaza, um einen attraktiven öffentlichen Platz als physische und metaphorische Verbindung zwischen Sculpture Park und Gebetsbereich zu schaffen – eine Passage vom Öffentlichen über das Halböffentliche zum Privaten. Der Gebetsbereich kombiniert traditionelle Elemente in einer modernen Interpretation. In der Form eines Quadrats – der perfekten Form, in der es keine Hierarchie zwischen den Einzelteilen gibt – symbolisiert sich die Kernidee des Islam, wonach in den Augen Allahs alle Menschen gleich sind. Die traditionelle Kuppel wird aufgeteilt in ein einzigartiges geometrisches Bogengeflecht. So entsteht ein Modul, das einen intimen und friedlichen, maßvoll von Tageslicht erhellten Raum schafft. Dieser spirituelle Bau wird ein prägnantes Element der Stadt und ein kraftvolles Wahrzeichen für die Gemeinschaft sein. Um die Privatsphäre der Menschen zu schützen, wird es zwei getrennte Flügel für Männer und Frauen geben. Die Bereiche für die Waschungen und Gebete sind ebenfalls durch eine Arkade mit traditionellen Maschrabijja-Gittern vom übrigen Teil des Komplexes abgetrennt. Ein stiller Garten mit einem Wasserelement als Symbol des Paradieses schließt den Außenbereich ab und bettet die Moschee in ein friedlich-ruhiges Umfeld. Ein traditionelles Gebäude in der Hauptstadt von Abu Dhabi wird mit diesem komplexen Entwurf zeitgenössisch interpretiert.

~ MUSEUM OF RELIGIOUS TOLERANCE
Ongoing

In an era where religion and its significance is being fundamentally questioned as it becomes a force for redefining moments in recent history, the proposed Museum of Religious Tolerance will be a groundbreaking project, promoting the principles of mutual respect and social responsibility. Destined to be a platform for rethinking, exploring, debating and corroborating the various paths of spirituality in order to achieve a deeper understanding, the building will include a museum, library, education centre and conference space, with a large outdoor events plaza. The structure itself is dematerialised – like the subject it represents – with a woven mesh skin that filters light during the day and becomes a twinkling jewel at night. The plaza becomes a treasure chest of Islamic teachings and literature carved and calligraphed into pedestals that people can walk by, read and study. At night the plaza is bathed in streams of light, the link between the sky and the earth, creating an evocative addition to Dubai's cultural offerings – that focuses attention of the city and steers its people towards a measure of introspection while elevating them from the routine of everyday life.

In einer Zeit, in der die Religion eine Kraft zur Neudefinition von Ereignissen der jüngeren Geschichte wird und sich dementsprechend grundlegenden Fragen zu stellen hat, ist das vorgeschlagene Museum of Religious Tolerance ein bahnbrechendes Projekt, das für die Grundsätze des gegenseitigen Respekts und der sozialen Verantwortung wirbt. Es soll die Möglichkeit bieten, die unterschiedlichen Wege von Spiritualität zu überdenken, zu ergründen, zu diskutieren und zu unterstützen, um zu einem tieferen Verständnis zu gelangen. Zu dem Gebäude gehören daher ein Museum, eine Bibliothek, ein Bildungszentrum und ein Konferenzsaal sowie eine große Plaza für Veranstaltungen. Die Konstruktion selbst ist gleichsam entmaterialisiert – wie das Thema, für das sie steht. Die Außenhaut aus einem Drahtgeflecht filtert das Tageslicht und lässt in der Nacht ein funkelndes Juwel erleuchten. Die Plaza wird zum Schmuckkästchen der islamischen Lehre und Literatur, kalligrafisch eingemeißelt in die Podeste, die zum Lesen und Studieren einladen. Auch bei Nacht ist die Plaza in helles Licht getaucht, die Verbindung zwischen Himmel und Erde, und wird damit eine weitere bedeutungsvolle kulturelle Attraktion Dubais, die auf die Stadt aufmerksam macht und die Menschen nach der Hektik des Tages wieder zu sich selbst führt.

~ THE WHITE HOTEL
Client: Al Qudra Real Estate
Storeys: 9
Ongoing

The brief for this hotel was to create a unique 5-star eco-resort that would be a focal feature of a masterplan for a vicinity in Abu Dhabi. The hotel design conveys an architectural identity that reflects the cultural architectural influences of the UAE translated into a contemporary form. Straddling the island bordering on Abu Dhabi City, the proposed crystalline structure reflects the calm, rippling water. The building's pure lines contrast with the flowing lines of Zayed bridge. An array of open spaces was created by using a complex arrangement of rectilinear faces. This myriad of planes fuses together to form rooms and balconies unique to each guest. The large openings frame spectacular views and bring a light and airy feel to the spaces within. The hotel core forms around a light-filled internal courtyard which can host a variety of facilities such as high-end boutiques, a spa and fine dining. Individual pixels within the façade were removed to create shafts of natural light. Activities spill out to the spacious platform deck – making an ideal location for gatherings or outdoor events. This shimmering hotel is a statement of minimalist design, a lighthouse with 360-degree views of Abu Dhabi's prestigious landmarks.

Das Bauprogramm für dieses Hotel forderte ein 5-Sterne-Resort mit ökologischer Ausrichtung, das ein zentrales Masterplanelement eines Stadtteils von Abu Dhabi werden soll. Der Entwurf vermittelt eine architektonische Identität, die die kulturellen baulichen Einflüsse auf die VAE in eine zeitgenössische Form übersetzt. Mit einem ausladenden Sockelbereich steht die kristalline Konstruktion, auf der sich die Wellen spiegeln, auf einer Insel und grenzt an Abu Dhabi City. Die klaren Linien bilden einen Gegensatz zu den fließenden Linien der Zayed-Brücke. Durch ein komplexes Arrangement rechteckiger Flächen entsteht eine Reihe offener Räume. Die vielen Ebenen verschmelzen zu individuellen Zimmern und Balkonen. Die großen Öffnungen rahmen spektakuläre Blicke und lassen die Innenräume lichterfüllt und luftig wirken. Der Hotelkern legt sich um einen hellen Innenhof, in dem sich unterschiedliche Einrichtungen wie Modeboutiquen, ein Wellnessbereich und Feinschmeckerrestaurants befinden. Einzelne Elemente wurden aus der Fassade genommen, um Tageslichtkanäle zu schaffen. Ein geräumiger Vorplatz wird zu einem idealen Ort für vielfältige Veranstaltungen und Events unter freiem Himmel. The White Hotel steht für minimalistisches Design und bietet wie ein Leuchtturm einen Panoramablick auf Abu Dhabis einzigartige Gebäudelandschaft.

ESSAYS

THE VERTICAL DREAM

At the end of 2009, the desert Emirate Dubai announced its inability to continue paying the interest due on its tens of billions of dollars of debt; and became the bogeyman of the global financial and economic arena as it were overnight. Share prices plummeted, construction giants downed tools, companies delayed their initial public offerings, and it seemed to be a new twist to the global financial crisis screw. Since saving face is one of the most important things in Islamic culture and incurring debt is considered illegal and immoral, it is easy to imagine how badly this news went down in the Gulf. Morale was at rock-bottom, the city appeared jaded, as if it had taken a direct hit. It was in need of financial support, and more besides; it was in need of resuscitation.

Just two months later, it became apparent that all was not lost for Dubai when in one of its central districts the Burj Khalifa, the tallest building in the world, opened. The inauguration date coincided with the fourth anniversary of Mohammed Al Maktoum's naming as regent Ruler of Dubai. Sheikh Mohammed is widely considered the architect of Dubai's modern renaissance and recently a key player in the crisis. The inauguration was intended as a sign that Dubai had not given up on its ambitious blueprint for a new form of urbanity for the future. In the run-up to the event, Dubai sceptics the world over were already indicating that the Burj would not pull the wool over their eyes. That they considered it nothing more than the old Guinness World Record ploy: Dubai, the Babel of the 21st century, and the Burj Khalifa, the new Tower of Babel. Their impressions seemed justifiable. Once the Gulf's metropolis admired worldwide for its city marketing, with its declaration of bankruptcy Dubai had gone and made a mockery of itself. The writing was definitely on the wall: Dubai was broke, once and for all – and together with this strange bubble in the middle of the Gulf, the dream of a new wonderful world of consumerism burst too. All of those projects convinced of their own gigantism would now gradually fall into isolation and be gently withdrawn from the desert region by their respective patrons. The term "Babel of the 21st century" is not however a reference to the tower or any of the other bold architectural feats that pepper the city. The Burj Khalifa represents a vertical dream of emancipation, which goes far beyond architectural designs and makes reference to the cultural and social development of the Emirate states. Dubai really is Babylon. With people from every corner of the world, from every religion and culture, with a share of immigrants of over 90% and the concept of a city, in which – up to now – traditional and modern nomads co-exist peacefully and with mutual aspirations and interests; Dubai is a social superlative. Surrounded by religious fanaticism and political instability, the state's attempt to create an open society on

Islamic foundations does indeed command our respect, despite all of its economic and social weak points. In our secular present the term Babel is in fact exclusively charged with negative connotations, and unjustifiably so. Babel can just as easily be interpreted as a story of emancipation.

For many people in Africa, Asia or the Arab world, the Gulf Emirates do indeed represent a story of emancipation. Dubai has developed into a symbol of social security and prosperity. After being condemned to poverty for millennia, Bedouin tried to shed the shackles of their old neo-colonial dependency and to establish a new, self-assured society. Dubai is a modernised, Islamic tribal society, whose ruler has to win over its people and persuade them to be part of the path he chooses into the future. As long as he does this successfully, he will achieve a strong identification with the modernisation project amongst the once-Bedouin Emirates. Today, if Western people and capital set up in Dubai, it is because they have been invited by the Emirates, not because the West wants it so. While Dubai may today seem like an imitation of our own culture, one should not be deceived by this. Strategists in the Gulf do not consider imitation as their aim but rather as an intermediary stage on the road to its own development. According to Dubai, "At some point, we want to encounter the West on an equal footing." So, the desert Emirate remains a role model for neighbouring states and repressed peoples. The old politics of neo-colonialism are replaced by a new sovereignty, which makes its own decisions on the country's development, such that over the past two decades, they have achieved a great amount in terms of progress. In a metaphorical sense, one could say that the economic crisis dealt Dubai its Babel-like punishment. But the Burj Khalifa is still standing nonetheless. The world will do well to continue taking an active interest in the fate of the Emirates.

[Michael Schindhelm]

DER VERTIKALE TRAUM

Ende 2009 kündigte das Wüstenemirat Dubai an, seine Zinsen auf Kredite in zweistelliger Milliardenhöhe nicht mehr zahlen zu wollen, und war mit einem Schlag der Buhmann der globalen Finanz- und Wirtschaftswelt. Aktienkurse purzelten, Bauriesen stellten ihren Betrieb ein, Unternehmen verschoben den Börsengang, die weltweite Krise schien sich weiter zu verschärfen. Da in der islamischen Kultur Gesichtswahrung fast über alles geht und Schuldenmachen als illegal und amoralisch gilt, kann man sich vorstellen, wie schlimm es am Golf stehen musste. Die Stimmung war auf dem Tiefpunkt, die Stadt schien ausgepowert und mitten ins Herz getroffen. Sie brauchte finanzielle Unterstützung, und mehr noch, so etwas wie einen Herzschrittmacher.

Dass Dubai nicht verloren war, zeigte sich schon zwei Monate später, als in einem zentralen Distrikt der Burj Khalifa eröffnet wurde, das höchste Bauwerk der Welt. Der Eröffnungstermin fiel auf den vierten Jahrestag der Regentschaft des Herrschers Mohammed Al Maktoum. Scheich Mohammed, der als der Architekt von Dubais Aufstieg und seit kurzem auch als entscheidender Akteur in der Krise galt. Die Inauguration sollte ein Zeichen dafür werden, dass Dubai den ehrgeizigen Entwurf einer neuen Form von Urbanität der Zukunft nicht aufgegeben hatte. Weltweit hatten Dubai-Skeptiker schon im Vorfeld zu verstehen gegeben, man lasse sich durch den Burj nicht beirren. Das sei doch wieder die alte Guinness-Rekord-Masche. Dubai, das Babel des 21. Jahrhunderts, und der Burj Khalifa als der neue Turm zu diesem Babel. Der Eindruck war berechtigt. Die einst für ihr Stadtmarketing weltweit bewunderte Metropole am Golf hatte sich mit ihrer Bankrotterklärung zum allgemeinen Gespött gemacht. Dubai sei nun endgültig abgebrannt, konnte man überall lesen, und mit der kuriosen Blase am Golf platze auch der Traum von der schönen neuen Konsumwelt. All die von Gigantismus zeugenden Projekte würden sich nun allmählich im Sande verlaufen und langsam von der Wüste zurückgeholt werden. Der Begriff des Babel im 21. Jahrhundert lässt sich aber nicht nur auf den Turm und die kühnen anderen Bauwerke der Stadt beziehen. Der Burj Khalifa repräsentiert einen vertikalen Traum von Emanzipation, der weit über Architekturentwürfe hinausgeht und auf die kulturelle und soziale Entwicklung der Emirate Bezug nimmt. Dubai ist tatsächlich Babylon. Mit Menschen aus aller Herren Länder, aus allen Religionen und Kulturen, mit einem Migrantenanteil von über 90 % und dem Konzept einer Stadt, in der sich bisher friedlich und im angestrebten beiderseitigen Interesse traditionelle und moderne Nomaden zusammenfinden, ist Dubai auch ein sozialer Superlativ. Umgeben von religiösem Fanatismus und politischer Instabilität, nötigt Dubais Versuch, eine weltoffene Gesellschaft mit islamischem Hintergrund aufzubauen, Respekt ab, allen wirtschaftlichen und sozialen Schwächen zum Trotz. Tatsächlich ist der Begriff von Babel ungerechtfertigterweise auch in unserer säkularen Gegenwart ausschließlich negativ besetzt. Babel kann aber genauso gut als eine Emanzipationsgeschichte gedeutet werden.

Für viele Menschen Afrikas, Asiens oder Arabiens sind die Emirate am Golf eine solche Emanzipationsgeschichte. Dubai hat sich zu einem Symbol von sozialer Sicherheit und Wohlstand entwickelt. Über Jahrtausende zur Armut verdammte Beduinen versuchen sich von der alten neokolonialen Abhängigkeit zu befreien und eine neue selbstbewusste Gesellschaft aufzubauen. Dubai ist eine sich modernisierende islamische Stammesgesellschaft, deren Herrscher das eigene Volk überzeugen und auf dem Weg in die Zukunft mitnehmen muss. Solange ihm das gelingt, erzielt er unter den einst beduinischen Emirati eine starke Identifikation mit dem Modernisierungsprojekt. Wenn heute Menschen und Kapital aus dem Westen in Dubai arbeiten, dann, weil sie von den Emirati eingeladen worden sind, nicht, weil der Westen dies initiierte beziehungsweise wollte. Wo Dubai heute aussieht wie eine Imitation unserer eigenen Kultur, sollte man sich nicht täuschen lassen. Nachahmung wird von den Strategen am Golf nicht als Ziel, sondern als eine Durchgangsstation der eigenen Entwicklung gesehen. „Irgendwann einmal", so heißt es in Dubai, „möchten wir dem Westen auf Augenhöhe begegnen". Damit bleibt das Wüstenemirat Vorbild für seine Nachbarn und unterdrückte Völker. Die alte Politik des Neokolonialismus wird abgelöst durch eine neue Souveränität, die selbst über die Entwicklung im Land entscheidet. Dabei ist in den letzten beiden Jahrzehnten vieles an Fortschritt erreicht worden. Im übertragenen Sinne könnte man sagen mit der Finanzkrise erfuhr Dubai seine Babel-Strafe. Der Burj Khalifa steht dennoch. Die Welt wird gut daran tun, weiter am Schicksal der Emirate Anteil zu nehmen.

[Michael Schindhelm]

DUBAI AND ABU DHABI: IDENTITY THROUGH IMAGERY, ISLANDS AND AN ARCHITECTURE OF EXTREMES

~ URBAN CLUSTERS

Dubai and Abu Dhabi display a preoccupation with the fabrication of a perceived image. The exploration of place through identity is a contemporary phenomenon. As technological advancements in the projection of unbuilt and newly built architecture become ever more sophisticated, the image becomes an end in itself, which can be instantaneously transmitted across the globe. Imagery of man-made coastlines and gravity-defying skylines or urban clusters is now portraying a form of urbanism that promotes new enclaves but also an exclusiveness. Reconnaissance technologies turn architecture into spectacle and a photogenic fantasy to drive investment and tourism. Dubai and Abu Dhabi are determined to transform themselves into perceived postcard perfect cities. Panoramas and imagery of unfinished projects give rise to the promise of fantasy. This is the future state of global urbanism – prescriptive and full of visual dramatisation. In effect, imagery is shaping Dubai and Abu Dhabi.

~ ISLANDS

The rulers of the UAE's coastal cities have long recognised water as the tool for survival – in trade and tourism as well as consumption. Major infrastructure projects to create new ports were first carried out in Dubai in the 1970s. More recently, new technologies and communications, regulations and infrastructures have brought about more dramatic morphological changes. The traditional Islamic horizontal urban composition and its direct relation to land and water have emerged in the form of geometric patterns and artificial islands. Flying over Dubai, one is confronted with a new type of urbanism which is seductively graphic and artificial. The city sprawls out like a three-dimensional algorithmic pattern: a geometric cityscape with over-scaled forms in endless variations. There is little difference between holiday accommodation and housing. Building programmes are blurred and undifferentiated. As a tourist there is no need to travel to distant, isolated destinations – islands are now close to shore, in a new typology of hydro-suburbia. The lowest form of spatial organisation, islands offer tremendous development potential, particularly as they offer a perceived exclusivity. The landscape and coastline is becoming developed to such an extent that it may soon be difficult to differentiate between the natural and the man-made. Artificial islands will add another 2,000 km of beachfront, in effect turning the Emirate and its coast into a resort whose constructed setting – like a stage set – provides manufactured scenarios of leisure and entertainment.

~ CONTRIVED CITIES

Urbanism in the Arab world has a remarkable precedent: historically, urbanising large areas and introducing a new aesthetic is very much inherent in the creation of the Arab city. Developers in the UAE are promoting a western lifestyle in glamorous settings to represent a perceived "high society" culture in the Gulf, living in exclusive towers, gated communities or exotic islands. These cities are an interpretation of urbanism which is predominantly sensual, spectacular, artificial and above all contemporary and global. Furthermore, the pastiche of the Islamic city shaped by Westerners to show an "indigenous" place – is ironically a major export, its imagery attracting millions of tourists seeking a seemingly authentic Arabesque city. In effect, what the global tourist might expect in the UAE has shaped the cities of Dubai and Abu Dhabi – and in return these new metropolises shape the world.

~ AN ARCHITECTURE OF EXTREMES

Dubai has become notorious for urbanising its land in a very specific way: taking a spatial approach that emphasises an enclave but also exclusiveness, so turning it into a zone. The city is effectively a cluster of mini-cities, rather like a metropolitan airport – an alchemy of parts put together by virtue of proximity. The abundance of infrastructure in major projects is so intense it forces a specific architecture to emerge. Such architecture is inevitably extreme, either too generic and anonymous or too iconic and extravagant. But in essence, it is well planned and interconnected. Similarly, the city is no longer an accumulation of invisible, hierarchical and commercial exchanges. There is something for everybody. Such networks of interconnected urban activities disguised under the overall portrayed image, and other references, make these UAE cities notable examples of problematic yet thriving 21st-century urban planning.

[George Katodrytis]

DUBAI UND ABU DHABI: IDENTITÄT DURCH VISUELLE INSZENIERUNG, INSELN UND EINE ARCHITEKTUR DER EXTREME

~ STÄDTISCHE CLUSTER

Dubai und Abu Dhabi sind sehr damit beschäftigt, eine bestimmte Wahrnehmung ihrer selbst durch die Öffentlichkeit herzustellen. Das Ausloten des Potenzials eines Ortes mittels Identitätsstiftung ist ein Phänomen unserer Zeit. Angesichts immer raffinierterer Technologien zur Visualisierung von ungebauten und neuen Gebäuden wird das Bild, das mit einem Klick global verbreitet werden kann, zum Selbstzweck. Bilder von künstlich angelegten Küstenlinien, atemberaubenden Skylines oder städtischen Clustern evozieren eine Form der Urbanität, die neue Enklaven, aber auch Exklusivität fördert. Moderne optische Präzisionstechnologie verwandelt die Architektur in ein Spektakel und in fotogene Fantasien zur Anlockung von Investoren und Touristen. Dubai und Abu Dhabi setzen alles daran, als perfekte Postkartenstädte zu erscheinen. Panoramen wie einzelne Bilder von noch nicht fertiggestellten Projekten versprechen immer neue Fantasien. Die Zukunft des globalen Städtebaus – präskriptiv und voller visueller Inszenierungen – kann hier besichtigt werden. Es sind die Bilder, die Dubai und Abu Dhabi ihre neue Gestalt geben.

~ INSELN

Die politischen Führungen der Küstenstädte in den VAE wissen seit Langem, dass das Wasser ihr wirtschaftliches Überleben sichert – es ist die Grundlage für Handel, Tourismus und eine moderne Konsumgesellschaft. Erste große Infrastrukturprojekte zur Errichtung neuer Hafenanlagen wurden in Dubai in den 1970er-Jahren initiiert. In jüngerer Zeit haben neue Technologien und Kommunikationsformen, neue gesetzliche Regelungen und Infrastrukturmaßnahmen einen dramatischen Wandel eingeleitet. Die traditionelle horizontale städtebauliche Komposition des Islam und die direkte Beziehung zu Land und Wasser tritt heute in Form von geometrischen Mustern und künstlichen Inseln hervor. Beim Betrachten Dubais aus der Luft, erkennt man einen neuen städtebaulichen Typus, der beeindruckend grafisch und entsprechend artifiziell ist. Die Stadt wächst wie ein dreidimensionaler Algorithmus: eine geometrische Stadtlandschaft mit überdimensionierten Formen in endloser Variation. Es gibt kaum einen Unterschied zwischen touristischen Vierteln und Wohnanlagen für Einheimische. Die Gebäudefunktionen sind kaum differenziert, Abgrenzungen nur schwach ausgeprägt. Der Tourist braucht nicht zu abgelegenen Zielen in der Ferne aufzubrechen – die Inseln liegen, gemäß der neuen Typologie einer Hydro-Vorstadt, direkt vor der Küste. Als niedrigste Form räumlicher Organisation bieten Inseln für die Objektentwicklung dennoch ein enormes Potenzial, vor allem weil sie als exklusive Orte gelten. Landschaft und Küste erreichen mittlerweile einen Erschließungsgrad, der es bald schwierig machen wird, zwischen der Natur und den Eingriffen des Menschen zu unterscheiden. Künstliche Inseln werden 2.000 km neue Strände schaffen und die Küsten in Ferienanlagen verwandeln, die wie Kulissen auf einer Bühne den Besuchern als Szenerie für diverse Freizeit- und Unterhaltungsaktivitäten dienen.

~ SYNTHETISCHE STÄDTE

Der Städtebau in der arabischen Welt blickt auf eine lange Tradition zurück. Geschichtlich gesehen sind eine dichte Urbanisierung großer Flächen und die Einführung einer neuen Ästhetik zentrale Elemente bei der Neugründung arabischer Städte. Die Immobilienfirmen propagieren einen westlichen Lebensstil in glamouröser Umgebung, der eine „High-Society-Kultur" mit exklusiven Hochhäusern, geschlossenen Wohnanlagen und exotischen Inseln suggeriert. In den neuen Städten manifestiert sich eine Interpretation des Städtebaus, die vor allem sinnlich, spektakulär und künstlich ist, aber zugleich zeitgenössisch und global. Der Pastiche einer islamischen Stadt – von westlichen Architekten mit dem Ziel gestaltet, einen Ort im „einheimischen" Stil zu schaffen – ist ironischerweise zu einem wichtigen Exportartikel geworden, dessen Symbolik Millionen von Touristen anzieht, die alle auf der Suche nach einer scheinbar authentischen arabischen Stadt sind. Es sind die Erwartungen der globalen Touristen, die Städten wie Dubai und Abu Dhabi ihre Gestalt verliehen haben, und diese neuen Metropolen geben nun ihrerseits der Welt eine neue Prägung.

~ EINE ARCHITEKTUR DER EXTREME

Dubai ist dafür bekannt, dass es seine Landflächen in sehr spezifischer Weise urbanisiert: Grundlage ist stets ein räumliches Konzept von Zonen mit enklavenartigem, aber zugleich exklusivem Charakter. Die Stadt ist im Grunde ein Cluster von Ministädten, wie ein großstädtischer Flughafen – eine Ansammlung von Teilen, die zusammengefügt werden, weil sie benachbart sind. Das Übermaß an Infrastrukturen bei Großprojekten erzeugt unweigerlich eine extreme Architektur, die entweder zu generisch und anonym oder zu ikonisch und extravagant ist. Trotzdem handelt es sich dabei im Wesentlichen um gut geplante und untereinander gut vernetzte Gebilde. Die Stadt ist nicht mehr eine Akkumulation von unsichtbaren, hierarchisch strukturierten oder kommerziellen Beziehungen des Austausches. Es gibt für jeden etwas. Netzwerke dieser Art, die aus diversen urbanen Aktivitäten zusammengeschaltet sind, sich aber hinter dem ausgegebenen Image und anderen für die Gesamtheit stehenden Zeichen verbergen, machen die Städte der VAE zu herausragenden Beispielen einer ebenso erfolgreichen wie problematischen Stadtplanung des 21. Jahrhunderts.

[George Katodrytis]

Urban Development, Dubai

Jumeirah Park, Dubai Masterplan

SUPERLATIVE URBANITY: THE UAE'S ADVENTURES IN SUSTAINABLE CITY MAKING

The UAE's ecological and natural environment – with its hot, arid climate and little arable land – makes it a formidable challenge for human habitation. Drinkable water is confined to a handful of oasis aquifers scattered across the predominantly desert terrain. Such conditions have never been particularly ideal for urban existence. Nonetheless, the Emirates have taken up the challenge of survival and progressed with courage, determination, deliberation and foresightedness, despite the numerous risks and hazards that come with such bold adventures.

Since its inception as an independent nation in 1971, the UAE has recognised the potential and value of urban development and has been committed to leading an urbanisation strategy to transform a series of small settlements into urban destinations of local, regional and international repute. This was propelled by the need to settle the Bedouin tribes, improve their quality of life, and ensure a commitment to achieving a population's critical mass to sustain an emerging state. Moreover, rising oil revenues (comprising 85% of the economy) provided an important prerequisite for grand visionary growth and development strategies and initiatives to expedite the transition towards a modern nation. Additional human capital became essential to support a fast-growing, diverse and robust development machine – made possible through attracting an increasing number of expatriate workers from around the world, making the UAE's population growth rate in the past decade one of the highest in the world. Concentrated in the cities, development has triggered an urban growth of exponential proportions, turning the previously small towns of Dubai, Abu Dhabi and Sharjah into sizeable urban centres of regional and global significance. Urban growth, however, brings challenges: how to reconcile problems of density, traffic, infrastructure, amenities and services, while maintaining economic prosperity, social equality and a better quality of life. Such challenges have been compounded with others – mostly environmental. Along with the emerging realities of globalisation, the UAE has embraced the "nothing is impossible" viewpoint and in a mere two decades has transformed itself into a modern country with remarkable regional and global clout. The current population of about 7.9 million represents a nearly sixteen-fold increase since the country's first census in 1975. Besides an impressive human development index and a remarkable economic growth rate, the UAE's per capita GDP/PPP ranks among the top five in the world. The UAE is (literally) aiming high, and thanks to increasing oil revenues combined with a visionary leadership, clearly the country is putting its money where its mouth is. Abu Dhabi is investing heavily in transforming the once-sleepy Bedouin settlement into a global economic, financial and cultural powerhouse. With such zeal topping the global charts, the fervent passion to build the best and most convenient cities should come as no surprise. The struggle to create an ideal home for its inhabitants, the striving to build better urban environments and the lust to attain superlative urbanity "have ultimately become key UAE aspirations". Two prime initiatives which best illustrate the country's determination particularly stand out: Masdar City and the Abu Dhabi Urban Planning Vision 2030.

~ MASDAR CITY

From the outset, Masdar City seemed an elusive, if not incomprehensible, proposition. Located at the outskirts of Abu Dhabi, this development is braced to be a showcase of a true "green city with renewable energy resources that emits zero pollution". Dubbed the "Silicon Valley of the Renewables", Masdar City is considered the first of its kind in the world. The city is conceived, initiated and developed by visionary decision makers, advised by world-class consultants – in a country whose entire economy, ironically, relies fundamentally on the extraction and export of the very same non-renewable fossil fuel energy that is the main contributor to a polluted, unsustainable global existence. Additionally, Masdar City is a unique enterprise in a country that reportedly has the highest per-capita footprint on the planet. According to the WWF's Living Planet Report (2010), the "Hummer nation" (where the 10-mile per gallon American SUV enjoys the largest global sales market second only to the US) has a less-than-impressive rate of resource consumption. If the world's 7 billion people emulated the UAE lifestyle and rate of consumption, they would need about four-and-a-half Earths to survive the rest of the 21st century. Envisaged as a global hub for a knowledge-based economy, comprising research and development, marketing and implementing alternative energy sources, Masdar City is one of the five-unit Masdar company aimed at diversifying the Emirate's economy through cultivating renewable energy and sustainable technologies. Masdar is a free zone that aims to attract global investment and enterprises. It brings the sustainability triad (social, economic and environmental) into a sophisticated, integrated and holistic synthesis. In terms of design, architect Norman Foster resolved to use reason and common sense: finding new ways to build in the stultifying heat by studying the way animals adapt to and exploit their environment. Rather like camels huddling together to create shade in the desert, Masdar City's urban design is based on the clustering of compact massing. Traditional Islamic cities in hot, dry regions also provided inspiration. Shaped by traditional socio-cultural imperatives, adaptive to local environmental and climatic conditions, and refined over time by trial and error, traditional urban fabric has proved to be a fertile ground for contemporary insight and innovation. Cities such as Fez, Damascus and Isfahan have provided a reference to re-examine, reinterpret and reinvent local architecture and urbanism to meet the demands of contemporary lifestyle necessities, quality of life and evolving tastes. The basics of passive energy design are found to be the most cost effective for creating a sustainable environment. The street network has a northeast /southwest orientation to reduce sun exposure and enhance natural ventilation. In addition to the compact, high-density massing, the design is focused on mixed-use zones of activities; narrow, walkable streets with maximum shading devices; open spaces with water fountains and sensible arid-climate landscaping. The pedestrian-friendly, car-free environment at street level will give residents the option of non-motorised transport (cycling and walking) or the use of an electric public transit network complemented with the world's first personal rapid transit vehicles – driverless pod cars that facilitate personal mobility across town. Individual building performance was carefully designed, based on combining thick walls with appropriate construction materials and insulation techniques; optimising natural light and the utilisation of low-energy-consuming devices; and aligning natural ventilation with the provision of efficient wind towers. Solar energy harvesting technologies, water consumption reduction techniques and waste treatment and recycling facilities are integrated to create a sustainable living environment, or what the architect Richard Rogers coins in his book "Cities for a Small Planet" a "circular metabolism city" where renewable inputs are balanced with reduced pollutants and waste.

~ ABU DHABI URBAN PLANNING VISION 2030
The 2030 Plan is another significant adventure in superlative urbanity. Not unlike Masdar City, it takes environmental concerns as central to an urban utopia. It lays out a set of standards that will transform Abu Dhabi into a vibrant, liveable, creative and sustainable city. The 2030 Plan combines ingenious urban and architectural design strategies with the use of clean technologies and renewable sources of energy. The ambitious and forward-thinking vision to manage long-term growth and development of the UAE capital has been developed by the progressive Abu Dhabi Urban Planning Council – a governmental organisation dedicated to driving and supporting the Emirate's urban development strategies. The outcome is a blueprint for a dynamic and inspiring urban setting. The UPC's aim for the plan is to "optimise Abu Dhabi's development through a 25-year programme of urban evolution. In doing so, it is laying the foundations for a socially cohesive and economically sustainable community that preserves the Emirate's unique cultural heritage". Seeking to re-create a people-oriented, authentic Arab city, the 2030 Plan is com-

parable with international masterplans of contemporary world cities, subscribing to the principles of Smart Growth that synthesises and applies to city making the sustainability triad of economic vibrancy, environmental sensibility, and social and cultural responsibility. It develops performance criteria for urban structure and urban design, environmental considerations, land use and density, connectivity and public open space, underscoring the significance of liveability, urban identity and image. Not unlike Masdar City, the plan prescribes to compact, dense, and mixed-use urban form; focuses on human scale, walkability and viable public spaces; and promotes multi-mode connectivity. It is a remarkable achievement not only for Abu Dhabi and the UAE – but for the entire Gulf region. For it boldly introduces and promotes an urban planning culture – something barely valued or understood in this part of the world. It upholds a commitment to the deliberate continuity, critical assessment and thoughtful evolution of traditional urban form and heritage. In addition, it proposes powerful and location-specific strategies for environmental protection (eg. coastal zoning, natural preserves, indigenous landscaping). Phasing and flexibility will accommodate continuous reflection, feedback, and improvement of the planning and urban outcome. Moreover, a detailed review process – including a public review – is constituted to ensure quality and diversity. Most significant of all is that in both its development process and on-going development, the 2030 Plan places public engagement and community participation in the planning process as key to the success and prosperity of the city. This is another first within the superlative urban adventure of the UAE.

The narratives of Masdar City and Plan 2030 are exemplary: both cases reflect the boundless ambition, fortitude, and determination of a people keen to make a meaningful contribution to human civilization. Because urbanity impacts how humans live, interact, and create, both projects can and will make significant contributions to the collective well-being of the people. Both make a remarkable contribution to a superlative UAE.

[Amer A. Moustafa]

Abu Dhabi Capital Plan 2030

STADTPLANUNG DER SUPERLATIVE: ÜBER DAS ABENTEUER, NACHHALTIGE STÄDTE IN DER WÜSTE ZU BAUEN.

Die natürlichen Gegebenheiten der VAE – heißes, trockenes Klima, wenige Ackerflächen – stellen für die Besiedelung durch Menschen eine Herausforderung dar. Trinkwasser gibt es nur in den Aquiferen weniger weit verstreuter Oasen. Städtischen Siedlungsformen stehen diese Bedingungen eher entgegen. Trotzdem haben die Emirate sich der schwierigen Aufgabe einer Urbanisierung der Wüste gestellt und sind mit Mut vorangeschritten, ungeachtet der zahlreichen Risiken, die ein solch kühnes Vorhaben mit sich bringt.

Die Einsicht in das Potenzial einer Urbanisierung des Landes setzte sich in den VAE schon bald nach Erlangung der Unabhängigkeit 1971 durch. Die Emirate verschrieben sich einer Entwicklungsstrategie, die aus einer Reihe von kleinen Siedlungen eine städtische Landschaft zu formen suchte, die lokale und regionale Funktionen übernehmen und zugleich internationale Bedeutung erhalten würde. Befördert wurde die Planung durch die Notwendigkeit, die Beduinenstämme sesshaft zu machen, ihre Lebensumstände zu verbessern und das für ein aufsteigendes Schwellenland benötigte Bevölkerungswachstum zu erzeugen. Die Öleinnahmen, die 85 % der Wirtschaft ausmachten, boten eine entscheidende Voraussetzung für diese visionären Planungen, die aus den Emiraten eine moderne Nation machen sollten. Das zusätzliche Humankapital, dessen es für eine rasche wirtschaftliche Expansion bedurfte, verschafften sich die VAE durch die Anwerbung von ausländischen Gastarbeitern. Die wirtschaftliche Expansion hat zu einem exponentiellen Wachstum geführt, das aus den einst kleinen Orten Dubai, Abu Dhabi und Sharjah urbane Zentren von bedeutendem regionalen und internationalen Gewicht gemacht hat. Rapides städtisches Wachstum schafft neue Herausforderungen: dichte Besiedelung, hohes Verkehrsaufkommen, die Bereitstellung von Infrastruktur und Versorgungseinrichtungen dürfen nicht die wirtschaftliche Prosperität, soziale Balance und Lebensqualität gefährden. Hinzu kommen Fragen der Umweltverträglichkeit. Der Globalisierung sind die VAE mit der Einstellung begegnet, dass „nichts unmöglich sei". In kaum zwei Jahrzehnten ist es ihnen gelungen, sich in ein modernes Land zu verwandeln, dessen Einfluss regional und international kontinuierlich zunimmt. Seit 1975 hat sich die Einwohnerzahl auf heute circa 7,9 Millionen fast versechzehnfacht. Neben einem ausgezeichneten Human Development Index und einem imposanten Wirtschaftswachstum gehören die VAE auch zu den fünf Ländern der Welt mit dem höchsten Bruttoinlandsprodukt und der höchsten Kaufpreisparität. Die Emirate wollen hoch hinaus und dank kräftig fließender Öleinnahmen und einer visionären politischen Führung lassen sie ihren Worten auch Taten folgen. Mit riesigen Investitionen transformiert Abu Dhabi gegenwärtig die einst verschlafene Beduinensiedlung zu einem internationalen Wirtschafts- und Finanzzentrum und auch zu einem kulturellen Drehkreuz. Angesichts des

Eifers, mit dem sich die VAE im Wettstreit der Nationen nach vorne schieben, ist es nicht verwunderlich, dass sie mit Leidenschaft die besten und effizientesten Städte bauen lassen. Das Bemühen, den eigenen Bewohnern ideale Wohnbedingungen in einer lebensfreundlichen städtischen Umgebung zu bieten und so eine Urbanität der Superlative zu ermöglichen, „gehört zu den zentralen Ambitionen der VAE".

Zwei Initiativen sind für die visionäre Zukunftsplanung der Emirate paradigmatisch: Masdar City und die Abu Dhabi Urban Planning Vision 2030.

~ MASDAR CITY

Der Plan für Masdar City schien von Beginn an schwer realisierbar, ja geradezu unverständlich zu sein. Als Vorzeigeprojekt konzipiert, soll am Stadtrand von Abu Dhabi eine „grüne Stadt mit erneuerbarer Energieversorgung ohne Schadstoffbelastung" gebaut werden. Oft als „Silicon Valley der erneuerbaren Energien" bezeichnet, gilt Masdar City als das erste Stadtplanungsprojekt dieser Art in der Welt. Konzeption, Initiative und Entwicklungspläne für die neue Stadt beruhen auf der Weitsicht und dem Mut von Entscheidungsträgern, die von renommierten Experten beraten wurden – ironischerweise in einem Land, dessen gesamte Wirtschaft von der Förderung und dem Export desjenigen fossilen Energieträgers abhängt, der einer der Hauptverursacher für eine umweltzerstörende Wirtschaftsweise ist. In einem Land, das pro Kopf die schlechteste CO_2-Bilanz weltweit hat, ist Masdar City ein einzigartig fortschrittliches Projekt. Der Ressourcenverbrauch der „Hummer nation" (VAE sind nach den USA das Land mit den höchsten Verkaufszahlen für den amerikanischen Geländewagen, der auf 100 km 23,5 Liter Benzin verschlingt) ist laut dem WWF Living Planet Report von 2010 alles andere als vorbildlich. Würden die 7 Milliarden Menschen auf der Erde dem Konsumniveau der VAE nacheifern, benötigten sie viereinhalb Erdplaneten, um allein durchs 21. Jahrhundert zu kommen. Als globale Drehscheibe für eine wissensbasierte Wirtschaft geplant, ist Masdar City eines von fünf Großprojekten der Masdar-Gesellschaft, deren Aufgabe die Diversifizierung der lokalen Wirtschaft durch die Entwicklung von nachhaltigen Technologien ist. Die Stadt ist eine sogenannte freie Zone, die Investoren und Unternehmen aus aller Welt anziehen soll. Die Triade sozialer, ökonomischer und ökologischer Nachhaltigkeit soll hier eine hochentwickelte und ganzheitliche Synthese erfahren. Norman Fosters Masterplan favorisiert Rationalität und die Orientierung am gesunden Menschenverstand: So wurde z. B. untersucht, wie die Tiere der Region sich ihrer Umgebung anpassen. Ähnlich wie Kamele in der Hitze zusammenrücken, um mehr Schatten zu werfen, sieht der Entwurf eine Konzentration von Gebäuden zu Clusterformationen vor. Eine weitere Inspirationsquelle waren alte islamische Städte in heißen, trockenen Regionen, deren über lange Zeiträume durch die Anpassung an soziale und kulturelle Gepflogenheiten und an die lokalen klimatischen Bedingungen entstandenen und nach der Methode Versuch und Irrtum optimierten Strukturen sich für den Entwurf ebenfalls als fruchtbar erwiesen. Städte wie Fez, Damaskus und Isfahan lieferten Vergleichsparameter für die Neuinterpretation der Tradition im Hinblick auf moderne Lebensgewohnheiten, Qualitätsstandards und ästhetische Bedürfnisse. Und ermöglichten so eine sicherere Einschätzung dessen, was eine regionsspezifische Architektur und Stadtplanung ausmachen sollte. Eine nachhaltige Stadt, so das Resultat, ließ sich am kostengünstigsten auf der Grundlage passiver Energienutzung erzielen. Das Straßennetz hat eine Nordost-/Südwest-Orientierung, um die Sonneneinstrahlung zu reduzieren und die natürliche Belüftung zu unterstützen. Neben einer dichten Bebauung mit kompakten Gebäuden favorisiert der Entwurf Zonen mit Mischnutzung, ferner enge, fußgängerfreundliche Straßen mit möglichst vielen Verschattungsvorrichtungen sowie offene Areale mit Springbrunnen und einer dem ariden Klima angepassten Garten- und Landschaftsgestaltung. Die autofreie Umgebung auf Straßenniveau ermöglicht es den Bewohnern, sich entweder zu Fuß, mit dem Fahrrad oder mit Hilfe eines elektrisch betriebenen öffentlichen Verkehrssystems fortzubewegen. Letzteres wird als Erstes auf der Welt aus automatisierten Einzelkabinen ohne Fahrer bestehen. Zur Verbesserung der ökologischen Gebäudeeigenschaften wurden dicke Wände mit geeigneten Baumaterialien und Isolierungen kombiniert, der natürliche Lichteinfall optimiert und energiesparsame Apparaturen verwendet. Mit gleicher Sorgfalt verzahnte man die natürliche Belüftung mit energieeffizienten Windkrafttürmen und installierte Anlagen zur solaren Energiegewinnung und zur Senkung des Wasserverbrauchs sowie umweltfreundliche Abfall- und Recyclingsysteme. Masdar City ist eine nachhaltige urbane Umgebung ganz im Sinne der Vision, die der Architekt Richard Rogers in seinem Buch „Cities for a small planet" als „Stadt mit einem zyklischen Metabolismus" beschreibt, in der zwischen der Zuführung von erneuerbaren Ressourcen und der Reduzierung von Schadstoffen sowie Abfällen ein ausgeglichenes Verhältnis besteht.

~ DIE „ABU DHABI URBAN PLANNING VISION 2030"
Der Rahmenplan für die Stadtentwicklung bis 2030 ist ein weiteres, geradezu abenteuerliches Projekt der Superlative. Ähnlich wie bei Masdar City haben bei diesem Entwurf eines urbanen Utopia Umweltbelange zentrale Bedeutung. Der Plan legt eine Reihe von Standards fest, die Abu Dhabi in eine kreative und nachhaltige Stadt mit hoher Lebensqualität verwandeln sollen. Innovative urbane und architektonische Entwurfsstrategien werden hier mit sauberen Technologien und der Erzeugung von erneuerbaren Energien kombiniert. Entwickelt wurde der Rahmenplan von dem progressiven Stadtplanungsrat von Abu Dhabi – einem staatlichen Gremium, dessen Aufgabe die Förderung der urbanen Entwicklung der Emirate ist. Ziel des

Stadtplanungsrats ist es, „die Entwicklung Abu Dhabis mit Hilfe eines auf 25 Jahre ausgelegten Programms der urbanen Entfaltung zu optimieren. Damit soll das Fundament für eine nachhaltige städtische Gemeinschaft gelegt werden, die zugleich den sozialen Zusammenhang fördert und das kulturelle Erbe der Emirate bewahrt". In ihrem Bemühen, eine an den Bedürfnissen der Bewohner orientierte, authentische arabische Stadt zu schaffen, lässt sich die Planungsvision mit den Masterplänen für andere große Weltstädte vergleichen, die sich ebenfalls den Prinzipien des intelligenten Wachstums verschrieben haben und die Forderungen der Nachhaltigkeitstriade erfüllen wollen: wirtschaftliche Dynamik, umweltgerechte Entwicklung, soziale und kulturelle Verantwortlichkeit. Der Plan für Abu Dhabi setzt Leistungskriterien für urbane Strukturen und architektonische Entwürfe, für ökologische Entscheidungen, Landnutzung und Bebauungsdichte sowie für die Verkehrsanbindung und die Gestaltung öffentlicher Freiräume. Dabei stehen Lebensqualität, städtische Identität und Imageförderung im Vordergrund. Der Plan schreibt eine kompakte und dichte urbane Form mit Mischnutzung vor, betont Überschaubarkeit, Fußgängerfreundlichkeit und attraktive öffentliche Räume und entwirft vielfältige Verkehrsanbindungen. Nicht nur für Abu Dhabi und die VAE, sondern für die gesamte Golfregion ist dies ein bemerkenswerter Erfolg, denn der Plan initiiert eine Form der Stadtplanung, für die es in diesem Teil der Welt bisher kaum Wertschätzung gab. Er ist einer bewussten Kontinuität verpflichtet, die kulturelles Erbe und überkommene urbane Formen gleichzeitig kritisch bewertet und aufmerksam weiterentwickelt. Ferner entwirft der Plan regionsspezifische Strategien zum Schutz der natürlichen Umwelt, z. B. die Einrichtung von Küstenzonen und Naturschutzgebieten oder einen an heimischer Fauna und Flora orientierten Landschaftsbau. Die Einteilung in Phasen und eine flexible Vorgehensweise ermöglichen fortgesetzte Reflexion und regelmäßiges Feedback. Ein detaillierter Bewertungsprozess, an dem auch die Öffentlichkeit teilnimmt, sorgt für die Sicherung von Qualität und Vielfalt. Von besonderer Bedeutung ist, dass die Planning Vision 2030 die Beteiligung der Bewohner am Planungsprozess als Schlüsselelement für ein Gelingen der Stadt ansieht. Unter den Superlativen der urbanen Großprojekte der VAE ist dies ein weiteres Novum.

Masdar City und die Abu Dhabi Urban Planning Vision 2030 haben Vorbildcharakter: Beide spiegeln den Ehrgeiz und die Entschlossenheit eines Volkes wider, das einen bedeutenden Beitrag zur menschlichen Zivilisation leisten will. In den Plänen wird dieses Streben manifest; sie verdeutlichen die Geisteshaltung und Arbeitsweise der VAE. Gerade weil die urbane Umgebung großen Einfluss auf die Lebensweisen, Interaktionsformen und auf die Kreativität ihrer Bewohner hat, besitzen beide Projekte das Potenzial, das Gemeinwohl des Landes und seiner Menschen entscheidend zu fördern und die VAE einmal mehr zu einem Land der Superlative zu machen.

[Amer A. Moustafa]

INDEX

ABU DHABI URBAN PLANNING COUNCIL
P. O. Box 62221
Abu Dhabi, UAE
www.upc.gov.ae

AEDAS LTD
19/F, 1063 King's Road, Quarry Bay
Hong Kong, China
www.aedas.com

TADAO ANDO ARCHITECT & ASSOCIATES
5–23 Toyosaki 2-Chome Kita-ku
Osaka 531–0072, Japan
www.tadao-ando.com

ARCHGROUP CONSULTANTS
P. O. Box 38390
Dubai, UAE
www.archgroupintl.com

ASYMPTOTE ARCHITECTURE
11–45 46th Avenue
New York, NY 11101, USA
www.asymptote-architecture.com

ATELIERS JEAN NOUVEL
10 Cité d'Angoulême
75011 Paris, France
www.jeannouvel.com

ATKINS
P. O. Box 5620
Dubai, UAE
www.atkinsglobal.com

DBI ARCHITECTURE
Level 1, 9 Trickett Street
Surfers Paradise Qld. 4217, Australia
www.dbidesign.com.au

DXB-LAB
P. O. Box 48878
Dubai, UAE
www.dxb-lab.com

FOSTER+PARTNERS
Riverside, 22 Hester Road
London SW11 4AN, Great Britain
www.fosterandpartners.com

GEHRY PARTNERS
12541 Beatrice Street
Los Angeles, CA 90066, USA
www.foga.com

GODWIN AUSTEN JOHNSON
Office 110, The Iridium Bldg.
P. O. Box 7185
Dubai, UAE
www.gaj-uae.ae

ZAHA HADID ARCHITECTS
10 Bowling Green Lane
London, Great Britain
www.zaha-hadid.com

GLENN HOWELLS ARCHITECTS
29 Maltings Place, 169 Tower Bridge Road
London SE1 3JB, Great Britain
www.glennhowells.co.uk

LAVA
Heilbronner Strasse 7
70174 Stuttgart, Germany
www.l-a-v-a.net

MASDAR CITY
P. O. Box 54115
Abu Dhabi, UAE
www.masdar.ae

OMA
Heer Bokelweg 149 AD
3032 Rotterdam, The Netherlands
www.oma.eu

ONL
Essenburgsingel 94c
3022 EG Rotterdam, The Netherlands
www.oosterhuis.nl

QUANTUM-AIP
P. O. Box 20956
Puerto Rico 00928
www.quantum-aiP. com

REISER + UMEMOTO
RUR ARCHITECTURE, PC
118 E. 59th Street, Suite 402
New York, NY 10022, USA
www.reiser-umemoto.com

RMJM
Floor 27, Monarch Office Tower
P. O. Box 6126
Dubai, UAE
www.rmjm.com

SCHWEGER ASSOCIATED ARCHITECTS
Media City Dubai
P. O. Box 24899
Dubai, UAE
www.schweger-architects.com

SOM
SKIDMORE, OWINGS & MERRILL, LLP
224 South Michigan
Chicago, IL 60604, USA
www.som.com

SMAQ
architecture urbanism research
Kastanienallee 10
10435 Berlin, Germany
www.smaq.net

ADRIAN SMITH +
GORDON GILL ARCHITECTURE
111 West Monroe, Suite 2300
Chicago, IL 60603, USA
www.smithgill.com

STUDIED IMPACT
Robert Ferry, Elizabeth Monoian
www.studiedimpact.com

TDIC
P. O. Box 126888
Abu Dhabi, UAE
www.tdic.ae

STUDIO PEI ZHU
B618, Tianhai Business Center
107 Dongsi Street
100007, Beijing, China
www.studiopeizhu.com

X-ARCHITECTS
Office No. 105 & 106
Bldg-47, DHCC, Al Karama
P. O. Box 111559
Dubai, UAE
www.x-architects.com

BIBLIOGRAPHY / LITERATURNACHWEIS

Abbas, Waheed:
UAE realty among first to recover in GCC.
Online article in: Emirates 24/7 Property. January 11, 2011
www.emirates247.com/property/real-estate/uae-realty-among-first-to-recover-in-gcc-2011-01-11-1.340676

Bellini, Oscar Eugenio and Laura Daglio:
New Frontiers in Architecture. Dubai between Vision and Reality. Vercelli 2010

Blum, Elizabeth and Peter Neitzke (Ed.): Dubai – Stadt aus dem Nichts.
In: Bauwelt Fundamente 143. Basel, Boston, Berlin, 2009

Bouman, Ole, Mitra Khoubrou and Rem Koolhaas (Ed.):
Volume/Al Manakh I. Amsterdam 2007

Business Monitor International:
United Arab Emirates Real Estate Report Q3 2010. June 3, 2010
www.marketresearch.com/Business-Monitor-International-v304/United-Arab-Emirates-Real-Estate-2700032/

Business Monitor International:
United Arab Emirates Real Estate Report Q2 2011. April 01, 2011
www.prlog.org/11411356-new-market-research-report-united-arab-emirates-real-estate-report-q2-2011.html

Central Intelligence Agency:
UAE Factbook, United Arab Emirates-History.
www.cia.gov/library/publications/the-world-factbook/geos/ae.html

Davidson, Christopher M.:
Abu Dhabi: Oil and Beyond. New York 2009

Davis, Mike and Daniel Bertrand Monk (Ed.):
Evil Paradises: Dreamworlds of Neoliberalism. New York, London 2008

Dubai Statistics Center:
www.dsc.gov.ae/En/StatisticalProjects/Pages/Projects.aspx

Elsheshtawy, Yasser:
Dubai: Behind an Urban Spectacle. London, New York 2010

Elsheshtawy, Yasser: The Evolving Arab City: Tradition, Modernity
and Urban Development. London, New York 2011

European Climate Foundation (Ed.):
Roadmap 2050. A practical guide to a propsperous low carbon Europe.
Den Haag 2010

Ghose, Gaurav (Ed.):
UAE Markets' Outlook for 2011.
In: Gulf News Online Newspapers. January 8, 2011
http://.gulfnews.com/business/markets/uae-markets-outlook-for-2011-1.742511

International Property Brokers Real Estate:
United Arab Emirates Market Report.
www.ipbre.com/countryProfile/United-Arab-Emirates/Market-Report

Jodidio, Philip:
Architecture in the Emirates. Cologne 2007

Kanna, Ahmed:
Dubai, the City as Corporation. Minnesota 2011

Kawach, Nadim:
UAE entering 2011 with signs of recovery from the clutches of 2008
Global Recession.
Online Article in: Dubai Stock Exchange. January 2, 2011
www.stockmarket-dubai.com/2011/01/uae-entering-2011-with-signs-of.html

Krane, Jim: Dubai:
The Story of the World's Fastest City. London 2009

Lindsay, Greg and John D. Kasarda:
The Aerotropolis Emirates. In: Aerotropolis. The Way We'll Live Next.
P. 287–325. New York 2011

National Bureau of Statistics, UAE
www.uaestatistics.gov.ae/EnglishHome/tabid/96/default.aspx

Reisz, Todd:
Volume/Al Manakh II. Golf Continued. Amsterdam 2010

Schöneberg, Gesa:
Contemporary Architecture in Arabia. Berlin 2008

United Nations Statistics Division
http://data.un.org/CountryProfile.aspx?crName=United%20Arab%20Emirates

PHOTO CREDITS / FOTONACHWEIS

GRATEFUL ACKNOWLEDGEMENTS TO:

BEHR CHAMPANA GAGNERON

GEORGE KATODRYTIS

AMER A. MOUSTAFA

SONIA MION AND NICOLA IANNIBELLO